THE INTEGRITY
OF THE BIBLE

*What We Should Know About the Development
and Legitimacy of the Bible*

by

Michael J. Chenevey

The Integrity of the Bible: What We Should Know About the Development and Legitimacy of the Bible

Copyright © 2017 by Michael J. Chenevey

This book is dedicated to my wife, Kristina,
for her persistence in keeping the vision of this work
in front of me.

CONTENTS

INTRODUCTION

The Purpose of This Book

Relationships are important. Think about a relationship with someone you are close to, for instance a mother or father, wife or husband. You want to know all about them; how they think on various subjects, where they came from, their background, and other details so you can know and understand them. You would be able to tell if, for instance, someone told you a friend or loved one said something that you knew to be out of their character. How would you know that? Because you knew that person well. It is the same with God. If we know Him, then we will know truth when we hear it and know when we hear from Him.

People hear God in many ways. Even though we may hear Him in some non-tactile ways, such as dreams, visions, prayer, still small voice, etc., the Bible, as God's primary revelation to us, is the only place where we can know the truth about Him. The Bible, as God's word, is truth (John 17:17). All truth that we hear audibly, perceptibly, or otherwise must conform to the words and concepts written in the Bible, and the more we know about the Bible and what the Bible says the better we will be able to discern that what we experience is from God or not.

> ### . . . Your Word
> ### is truth.
> #### John 17:17

The written and carefully transmitted words of God are the only authoritative evidence that anyone has for specific truth about the LORD[1]. We can learn just so much about God, His character, and plans from nature, which is referred to as "general revelation" by theologians, and by other means such as prayer, hearing preaching or conversations, books other than the Bible, etc., but it is in the Bible that we can clearly read about Him, what He has done, is doing, will do, and what He asks of us. The Bible is revelation, and as such is sufficient for the most important things we need to know about the LORD. All true things that we know about God the Father, God the Son, Jesus, and God the Holy Spirit come from the Bible.

The Bible's content is paramount to faith, of course. What is also important is to understand and appreciate how the Bible came together. People who are interested in the Bible have many questions about it outside of its content. Now we come to the primary subject of this book. This book addresses things Bible readers and inquirers want to know about the development of the Bible itself: its transmission through time, the languages and cultures behind it, the authoritative list of books contained in the Bible, what original Bible writings are still available to us today, scientific approaches to understanding the content and translation, why we have so many types of translations, and which are helpful for different types of understanding.

Understanding both the Bible's development and its content is important to every person of faith. We all need to know, understand, and apply what the inspired authors actually wrote, in context, and understand what God intends for us to learn from it. In order to help us address our inquiries, we can benefit from an understanding of the development of the Bible itself; how did we get these particular books and words passed down to us in the first place?

Do Christians need to understand all of the technical details about the development of the Bible in order to understand and apply its content? No, of course not. People can drive cars without needing to know how engines or transmissions work, or even how they are maintained. Just as with cars, which require specially trained mechanics to ensure they function properly, it is important that we have what could be called "mechanics" or "technicians" of the faith in the church. These are those specially trained people who understand the historical and technical details about the Bible, and

---

[1] I will refer to the "LORD" throughout this material, because English translators have consistently used this designation for the God of the Hebrews. The Hebrew name is holy (not to be pronounced), referring to four consonants of the Hebrew alphabet that designate the Hebrew and Christian God from other gods or lords. The four letters are referred to by scholars as the "tetragrammaton" (See more about this in Chapter 3). The divine name is transliterated in English as "YHWH." He is sometimes referred to by Jews as "adonai," which means "Lord" in the general sense in Hebrew.

who can faithfully relate knowledge and understanding to non-technical people so the latter can better understand their Bible and solidify their faith.[2]

Why is it helpful to know this material? In order to keep our Christian faith orthodox,[3] i.e., sound doctrine,[4] adhering to the "faith once delivered,"[5] and to honor the understanding of the faith that was literally fought over and decided millennia ago by learned and inspired men and women. In fact, we are still fighting against heresies, or deviations from the truths of the Bible, that were dealt with vehemently in the first centuries of the Christian Church. Among these deviations are Jehovah's Witnesses, who believe similarly to the ancient Arians,[6] or others such as Universalists (e.g., Unity and Unitarian churches), or the Latter Day Saints ("Mormons"), who don't believe Jesus is unique. There's truly nothing new under the sun when it comes to those who would deviate from orthodox Christianity.[7] We will explore this latter concept further in the next section.

IMPORTANCE OF UNDERSTANDING THE BIBLE: THEOLOGY & PRACTICAL APPLICATION

As we discussed above, the Bible is the only tangible way we know truth about God. The truths we learn by studying the Bible and its development are foundational to our understanding of God, and this understanding is what we call our theology. The word "theology" may bring all sorts of things to mind, e.g., dry, boring, irrelevant, or technical, but our theology is simply what we believe about God, or what we think God tells us in the Bible about any topic. Everyone, including atheists, have a theology. Some may argue that there is no agreed upon theology for Christians. However, this is not true. There is one place where the fundamental Christian theology elements

---

[2] See Eph. 4:11-14

[3] 1 Tim. 4:16, 2 Tim. 3:15-17, 2 Cor. 13:5 ("Examine (or test) yourselves, as to whether you are in the faith" *Author's translation* – the measure is the Words of God, the Bible).

[4] 2 Tim 4:1-3

[5] Jude 1:3b

[6] Arians were followers of Bishop Arius in the 3rd and 4th centuries AD, who taught that Jesus was a lesser, created being, not equal with God.

[7] The essence of the orthodox Christian Faith has been expressed succinctly in the Nicene Creed, See Appendix A

exist, what many would term "orthodox" in the sense that it contains the essential elements that all people who call themselves Christian must believe. The Christian Church as a whole has agreed that the concepts written in the Nicene Creed (developed at the Council of Nicea in 325 AD) are the most fundamental for Christianity. See Appendix A for the content of this creed. Each of the concepts in the creed are found in the Bible.

Our lives and important decisions are based on the Bible, as God's words to us. What we do, our acts and decisions, are a result of what we believe. As we seek to live by our convictions, we need to understand the "why" behind our beliefs, not just copy them from others, even those who we might greatly respect. This understanding is accomplished by study and critical dialog with others who are seeking to understand the Bible and faith, and most importantly, living out our faith and encouraging others from our own study and experiences.

CHAPTER 1
TRANSMISSION: THE SPOKEN, WRITTEN, AND PRINTED WORD

INSPIRATION

Christians believe that the Bible is the LORD's words to His people. The writers were inspired, or "breathed in" the words by the Holy Spirit,[8] and wrote in their own language, cultural setting, and in their own hand the words the LORD wanted His people to know about Him and what He wanted for and from them.[9] For the New Testament, the authors wrote down what Jesus (Hebrew, *Yehoshua*[10]) said while He was ministering in person on the earth, or they wrote about issues confronting the early church. In some cases, the New Testament authors were protégés or contemporaries of those who walked with Jesus, so they were writing an authoritative account of early Christian activities and understanding of the faith. Note that Mark (or John Mark) was a disciple of Peter's[11] as well as Paul's.[12] Luke was a companion of Paul's.[13] Luke is possibly the only non-Jew who wrote any part of the New Testament.[14]

> ### **Did You Know?**
>
> Jesus' name in Hebrew is Yehoshua. In Greek, it's Iesous (pronounced, "ee-ay-sous"), and both mean "Yah is Salvation"

---

[8] 2 Tim 3:16-17, 2 Peter 1:21

[9] Rom 15:4

[10] Iesous is the Greek form of the Hebrew, Yehoshua (In English, Joshua), which is derived from two words, "YHWH" (Strongs 03068), the divine Name and "Yasha" (Strongs 03467), meaning "to save or deliver." Yehoshua means, "The LORD is salvation." Some use the contraction Yeshua or Y'shua, which in Hebrew means "salvation" but this removes something important from the original Hebrew meaning of the Jesus' name, which includes the Divine name, or Tetragrammaton.

[11] As explained by Papias (an Early Church Father, AD 60-140), as quoted in Eusebius of Caesarea, Historia Ecclesiastica, in Philip Schaff's Early Church Fathers series, Nicene and Post-Nicene Fathers, Series II, Volume I, Book II (Peabody, MA: Hendrickson, 1994).

[12] Acts 12:25

[13] 2 Tim 4:11, Philemon 1:24

[14] Both the Roman and Eastern churches believe Luke was a gentile convert

THE HEBREW CONTEXT MATTERS

The words in the entire Bible were written down by Hebrew[15] people in a Hebrew context. Most scholars agree that the New Testament was written by Jewish authors, not gentiles although as stated above, possibly Luke was a gentile convert. Jesus the Messiah[16] was a Jew, and lived as an Orthodox Jew. His Gospel message was Jewish, directed to a Jewish audience. Many Christians read only the Newer Testament, and neglect the Older Testament. However, the gospel of the New Testament is based on the Old Testament. The messianic promise is given in the Old Testament. The Old Testament, specifically the Greek translation called the "Septuagint,"

> **Did You Know?**
>
> The original Bible manuscripts (both Old and New Testaments) did not have any chapter or verse markings

which will be addressed more later, is quoted every time the Greek word "Scripture"[17] is used in the New Testament. The New Testament is an understanding of God based on, or derived from, the "Older" Testament. The New Testament proceeds from the Old Testament. The New Testament is a theology of the Old Testament. They naturally go together. Christians cannot just read the New Testament; they must understand its context by understanding the Old Testament and the Hebrew story.

ABOUT TRANSMISSION: HANDWRITTEN AND COPIED, AND PRINTED

We know that the Bible was derived from a middle-eastern culture. It was originally written in several languages. The Hebrew Scriptures, what Christians today refer to as the Old Testament is easy to put into a Hebrew context, since it was written by and for Hebrew people. For the New Testament, it might be helpful to think about the original hearers of the teachings of Jesus. Many times the majority of them were

---

[15] When not discussing language specifically, I will use the terms "Hebrew(s)," "Jewish," and "Jews" synonymously throughout this book to refer to the people of Israel (i.e., descendants of the twelve sons of Jacob) in a general cultural sense.

[16] Transliterated "*Mashiach*" in Hebrew and "*Christos*" or Christ in Greek

[17] The Greek word for Scripture is *graphe* = "writing"; it refers to "Scripture" in the correct context only.

Hebrew, or Jewish. Their native tongue was most likely Hebrew or Aramaic,[18] a derivative of Hebrew. In the minds of the New Testament writers, they thought in Hebrew and most likely they heard the words in Hebrew or Aramaic originally, too, and then wrote in the common Greek language of the day.

At various times in history, and for great lengths of time, the Hebrews did not actually autonomously rule their homeland, or even live in the geopolitical region we know today as Israel, so they had to translate their Scriptures into the language or languages of the cultures in which they lived. The scattering or dispersion of the Jewish people geographically is what is called the "Diaspora."[19] The people of various ethnic groups, called *ethnos* in Greek or "nations" as we often read it in English, refers to the various cultures into which Jews went in the various Diaspora events (e.g., Acts 2:5-11).

BIBLICAL MEDIA

Biblical material was originally hand-written and subsequently hand-copied onto various media by trained scribes who specialized in language and the copying craft. This manual effort was the primary process of transmission and preservation of the Bible until around 1440 AD, when Johannes Gutenberg invented the first printing press with movable type.

Prior to printing on paper, ancient media for biblical writings included papyrus and parchment, among other things.

Papyrus is a medium derived from the stem part of the papyrus plant, and was originally used for writing media in ancient Egypt. It has also been used for various purposes including writing media around the Mediterranean Sea, where the plant grows.

---

[18] We will discuss Aramaic as a language of the Bible later, but for now we can say it was an early Semitic language of the middle east, commonly used at the time of Jesus and the early church

[19] The first diaspora happened in the 8th century BC when the Assyrians defeated the northern tribes of Israel and dispersed them across their wide empire (See 1 Chronicles 5:26, 2 Kings 15:29); this was the first of many deportations Israel, and eventually Judah in the South, would experience.

An original parchment scroll of a portion of the Hebrew Scriptures. Source: the Israel Antiquities Authority 1993; photographer not named, Library of Congress (Public Domain)

Parchment is a finely scraped animal skin, typically from goats, sheep, or cattle.

Vellum is similar to parchment, but specifically produced from calfskin.

Ancient media for Bible manuscripts have also included wood and rock carvings (think of Exodus 31:18).

VARIOUS FORMS

The writers also employed various forms for presenting or binding the written material, including:

- Scrolls, which were rolled parchment or vellum. This is the traditional form of the Hebrew Scripture.
- Codex, which is the book form, has been in use since 1st c AD.
- Tablets were the oldest form of presentation.

by, Michael J. Chenevey

AGE OF PRINTING

Printing presses using moveable type produce some level of consistency in replicating and proliferating works of literature. However, with regard to the Bible, along with automation came a variability in quality. Moveable type allowed variation in the types and ways of printing, as well as a proliferation of the number of printers who could produce Bibles on demand. Some of these printers were very diligent and devoted, and others were less so. We see slight deviances between printed versions of the Bible that originated from different locations.

A famous example of a printing error is in the so-called "Wicked Bible," published

The glaring "typo" from the "Wicked" Bible, Exodos 20:14. Image is not copyrighted due to the age of the work.

in 1631 by Robert Baker and Martin Lucas, the royal printers in London. This printed Bible contained a flagrant error:

Perhaps what George Abbot, the Archbishop of Canterbury, wrote sums up the printing industry of the 17th century,

"I knew the time when great care was had about printing, the Bibles especially, good compositors and the best correctors were gotten being grave and learned men, the paper and the letter rare, and faire every way of the best, but now the paper is nought, the composers boys, and the correctors unlearned."[20]

---

[20] Ingelbart, Louis Edward (1987). Press Freedoms. A Descriptive Calendar of Concepts, Interpretations, Events, and Courts Actions, from 4000 B.C. to the Present, p. 40, Greenwood Publishing.

In the age of manually-composited printing, there have been a number of Bible editions that contained compositing errors; at least 27 instances have been recorded from 1549 to 1944.[21]

Today's digital bibles used for both print and digital formats are highly quality-controlled because of the many safeguards that exist in the replication and printing process. The printing and replication issues such as those described above are rare or perhaps nonexistent today.

---

[21] One list of compositing errors can be found online at Wikipedia: https://en.wikipedia.org/wiki/Bible_errata

CHAPTER 2
AN OVERVIEW OF THE CANON

INTRODUCTION TO THE CANON

I n the second century AD, Christians started referring to the Jewish Bible as the "Old Testament" and to the apostolic writings or Scriptures as the "New Testament." The term "testament" in English refers to the Greek concept of "covenant." The Greek word is *diatheke*, which means settlement or agreement.

The canon, which means "reed" or "measuring rod," is simply the list of books that the apostolic Church considered authoritative. The church today consists of a variety of different groups, all of whom have claimed apostolic foundations: the Eastern or Greek Church primarily represented by the Orthodox union of churches, which claim Constantinople, or modern Istanbul, Turkey as their historical center,[22] the Roman Church or the Western or Latin church, represented by the Roman Catholic denomination which claim Rome as their historical center, the Ethiopian Orthodox Tewahedo Church, which claims heritage back to Solomon and his relationship with the Queen of Sheba[23] as well as visits from the Apostle Matthew,[24] the Indian (Nasrani) Orthodox Church, centered in Kerala, India and which was founded by the Apostle Thomas,[25] the Armenian Orthodox Church, which was founded by the Apostles Bartholomew and Thaddeus, and the various branches that split from the above,

---

[22] The Church or denomination that has been called "Orthodox" since the "Great Schism" split with Rome in 1054 AD has a number of apostolic-founded locations, including four of the five original "sees" which were (and are) overseen by "Popes": Constantinople (modern Istanbul), Jerusalem, Antioch (in modern Turkey), and Alexandria (Egypt). The fifth see was (and is) Rome, under the leadership of its patriarch or Pope, within the Church or denomination called "Catholic" since the Great Schism.

[23] Modern Ethiopia is a possible provenance for the Queen and it is claimed that from the same country came the eunuch we read about being baptized as a Christian in Acts 8:27. Early evangelist and church father John Chrysostom states that there were Ethiopian Jews present during the Acts 2:38 event: Meskel and the Ethiopians. EOTC Publication Committee, September, 2015.

[24] Socrates and Sozomenus Ecclesiastical Histories, Historia Ecclesiastica, in Philip Schaff's Early Church Fathers series, Nicene and Post-Nicene Fathers, Series II, Volume II (Peabody, MA: Hendrickson, 1994). p. 57

[25] The Jews of India: A Story of Three Communities by Orpa Slapak. The Israel Museum, Jerusalem. 2003. p. 27.

including the modern Protestant groups, Pentecostals, and the plethora of Independent churches. Appendix B shows the original and derivative Christian groups as they developed over time.

Given the great diversity of the church today, there is likely no way to reach any consensus on canonical matters, even if that was of interest. We must go back to the first few centuries of the Christian Church, when it existed under one name, albeit with regionalized leadership, and was comprised of those who were closer in time to Jesus and the apostles and their immediate successors in order to learn about the authoritative canon. We will learn more about these things in the next couple chapters on the canon.

It is important to understand that there are generally no disputes today among Christians as to which books should be included in the New Testament, nor has here been any significant dispute about the New Testament canon since the 16th century Reformation era. We will discuss the details later, but for our overview, it is important to understand that we know from the Muratorian Canon (or Fragment) that the 27 books of the New Testament canon have been consistent since before 190 AD. In 367 AD, Bishop Athanasius lists all 27 books of the New Testament as we have them today in his Thirty-ninth Festal Letter.[26]

Christian groups differ over the Old Testament canon. Appendix C shows the canonical books of the Old Testament in use among the various Christian groups around the world and how they differ. This dispute originated in the Jewish community, about three hundred years before the advent of Jesus. The issues are really about the Hebrew canon. It turns out that a few hundred years before the advent of Jesus, Hebrew scholars added a few additional books to their Scriptures that were

> ## Did You Know?
>
> Some Old Testament books were marked by the letters of the Hebrew alphabet for oral readings (e.g., Isaiah)

written in the *lingua franca* of the day, namely Greek and Aramaic. In dispute is the question as to whether these additional books are inspired or just helpful reading. We will discuss this situation and how it came about next. The discussion revolves around language and manuscript evidence.

---

[26] F.F. Bruce, The Canon of Scripture, (Downer's Grove, IL: InterVarsity Press, 1988), P.209

CHAPTER 3
THE OLD TESTAMENT,
OR THE HEBREW BIBLE

by, Michael J. Chenevey

PRIMARY LANGUAGES
HEBREW

The Old Testament was originally written primarily in the ancient Hebrew language. We call it "ancient" because the language as recorded in the Hebrew Scriptures is not the same as what modern Hebrew speakers and writers use. One characteristic both the modern and ancient versions have in common is that Hebrew has always been a consonantal language; no vowels, and reads from right to left, contra English. The Hebrew Bible is sometimes called the Tenach (or often Tenakh), an abbreviated form of the three Hebrew words used to describe its parts: Torah (the Law, or the first five books of the Old Testament), Nevi'im (The Prophets), and Ketuvim (the Writings; "K" and "Ch" are interchangeable in the transliteration for the eighth Hebrew letter, *Het*). The use of Hebrew is important for the Jews of course, because this is their native tongue. However, the situation is challenging from a textual point of view, because the best original hand written extant[27] versions of Hebrew manuscripts are relatively late, from 800 AD and later. This is very late compared to the Dead Sea Scrolls from the 2nd c BC and the earliest Greek translations from the 4th and 5th c AD that we have in hand.

We will dive deeper into the subject of manuscript reliability later as well, but it is important that the student of ancient handwritten and hand-copied Hebrew manuscripts understand the level of the quality control that went into the process. Each Hebrew sofer (scribe) literally counted every letter, every word, and understood how many should be on each section of the scrolls.[28] They marked the central word and letter in each book. These central words are placed in larger font type in the *Biblia Hebraica Stuttgartensia* (BHS), which is the primary printed edition of the Hebrew "Masoretic" biblical text available today. We will discuss the Masoretic text and the Masoretes later, under the section describing manuscript evidence. For instance, the

---

[27] Extant means the ones we can figuratively "put our hands on" today.

[28] Although we are discussing the ancient copying process, it is important to understand that handwritten Hebrew is still the only kosher way of producing a Hebrew Torah (first five books of the Law) even today. Contemporary Jewish scribes produce each "Sefer Torah" (Book of the Law) with the same or similar process and care as has been done for thousands of years.

middle letter of the Torah is the *vav* (in this case, the Hebrew "O") in the word translated as "belly" in Leviticus 11:42.

Modern scribes tell us the Sefer Torah (literally, "Book of the Law") has 304,805 letters. One source says the Torah scrolls, as used today, have a 0.00004% difference, which amounts to six letters in question.[29]

"The scholars counted the words and consonants of each book, the middle word and middle consonants, the peculiarities of script, etc. Even when such peculiarities were clearly due to error or to accident, they were perpetuated and interpreted by a mystical meaning. Broken and inverted letters, consonants that were too small or too large, dots which were out of place — all these oddities were handed down as God-intended"[30]

One Jewish source explains that one driver behind the quantification of the texts (words, letters) was for accounting purposes; the copyists were paid for the work they did, and the means to justify payment was by the number of letters written.[31]

THE DIVINE NAME IN HEBREW

This is a good place to discuss the divine name and its importance in the scribal process. We all need to understand that the Hebrew and Christian God has a particular name, and it is not the general "God," or "Lord," or any of the other names that are descriptive of His character. Some point to adjectival names such as *rapha*, the healer, *nissi*, the banner, *El Shaddai*, the sovereign provider, *Elohim*, majestic God, etc., but as stated above, these are merely descriptive terms that explain what the LORD was doing in specific circumstances. His name is unique, and it is Hebrew. It is spelled YHWH or YHVH. This is a transliteration using English letters, not the actual Hebrew, of course. In many English translations the name is spelled using upper case or small capital letters, as LORD. As stated earlier, Hebrew is a consonantal language, so there are no vowels. The name was only pronounced orally. The divine name is holy and has always be treated in a reverential way by the Hebrew people. The Jewish people since pre-Christian times have not pronounced the name, and it would be a good thing if Christians also held it with similar reverence. Since the Jews long ago stopped

---

[29] From the website, http://scrolls4all.org/scrolls/the-scribe/

[30] http://www.newadvent.org/cathen/09627a.htm

[31] http://www.jewishencyclopedia.com/articles/10465-masorah. It is interesting to note that the scribes today require approximately one year to hand write a full Torah. Estimations on timing include one sheet per week, 7-8 minutes per line, 4 letters per minute. They can be valued at upwards of $50,000 USD each.

pronouncing "The Name" ("HaShem" in Hebrew[32]), its true pronunciation has been lost. Jews typically substitute the word, "adonai" which means "lord," in a general sense.

Scribes who are copying Scripture by hand (which is still done today all around the world, by the way) have a specific ritual they perform when they write the divine name. They first immerse in, or are "covered with" water for a spiritual cleansing. This body of water is called a mikvah. It looks sort of like a small spa. You will find mikvaot (plural) in modern scriptoriums as well as ancient ones. It is well known that the Pool of Siloam, described in John 9:7, 11 was a mikvah,

The divine name of the Lord, in Hebrew (What is called the Tetraarammaton)

used for ceremonial cleansings prior to and during festivals and religious activities in Jerusalem. After the ritual cleansing, the scribes wipe their pen or use a new one, then write the divine name slowly and carefully, while pondering its significance.

We will address the use and importance of Hebrew in other parts of this material, but suffice it to say that, although it was the original language used for the oldest parts of the Bible, and it is considered the only authorized biblical language for modern orthodox Jews, the extant manuscript evidence for much of our Old Testament today is very late, dating from the ninth century, AD. Modern translators tend to use manuscripts that are much older than the oldest Hebrew writings we have available today and weigh them more heavily, even though these older manuscripts are all Greek translations of Hebrew. This situation with manuscripts is why in many modern translations, such as the New International Version, the translators insert notes now and then explaining their use of the "earliest and most reliable manuscripts." They are referring to the older extant Greek manuscripts of the Old Testament from the fourth and fifth centuries, AD.

---

[32] A good discussion on "HaShem" ("the name" in Hebrew) can be found in the Jewish Encyclopedia online: http://www.jewishencyclopedia.com/articles/14346-tetragrammaton

ARAMAIC

Some parts of the Hebrew Bible are written in the Aramaic language (about 250 verses out of 23,000). What is Aramaic? It was the Semitic *lingua franca* of the seventh and sixth centuries, BC, and common to various people groups including the Babylonians and Persians. During the Babylonian exile, the Jews spoke this language.

The Aramaic parts of the Bible are found in the works which were written during and after the Babylonian exile. The primary books containing Aramaic are Daniel and Ezra. The entire section, from Daniel 2:4 to 7:28 is written in Aramaic. The phrase, "*Mene Mene Tekel Upharsin*" from the "writing on the wall" section in Daniel 5:25 is an Aramaic expression.

> **Did You Know?**
>
> The Hebrew Psalms contain 116 more verses than Christian Bibles. The Hebrew Bibles count the ascriptions.

GREEK

While the Old Testament was written originally in Hebrew and Aramaic, it is important to understand that the best extant manuscripts of the ancient Hebrew Bible are actually written in Greek, from translations made by Jews during the Hellenistic (Greek-cultured) pre-Christian era. The most important Greek translation of the Hebrew Bible was written around 250 BC, and is called the "Septuagint" (Greek for 70) or LXX, Latin numerals for 70.

SEPTUAGINT OR LXX

The Greek translation of the Hebrew Bible is very important, since it is represented in the oldest and most complete ancient manuscripts we have of the Old Testament. The LXX met the needs of the Hellenized Jews in the ancient world. However, the LXX is also very important to Christians. The oldest extant full copies are from circa 300 AD, and parts of the Hebrew Scripture are represented in the Dead Sea Scrolls, dated 300 BC -100 AD. As such, the LXX is actually more reliable than the Hebrew versions we have today. Legend surrounds the origin of the LXX. Some parts of the legend seem embellished, while others no doubt tell us some true things about the origin of the LXX.

The source of the origin story comes from a second century BC author, Aristobulus, in his *Letter of Aristeas.* The Aristobulus account was also repeated by Flavius Josephus[33] and Philo of Alexandria,[34] both first century Jewish writers. In the *Letter*, it is explained that the LXX story begins with the King of Egypt, Ptolemy II Philadelphus (287-47 BC). He had completed his magnificent library in Alexandria and desired to include a copy of the Hebrew Scriptures translated into Greek. He requested a copy of "The Law" from Eleazar, Chief Priest in Jerusalem. Eleazar complied and sent six translators from each of the twelve tribes of Israel to Egypt to do the translation work. The number of translators varies from account to account; some say seventy-two, some say seventy, and others, seventy-five. As well, the actual texts that were translated varies. Most agree that the Torah (first five books, or the Pentateuch) was translated initially, and later the others were added until the Egyptian library had the entire Hebrew Scriptures. The work of translation, according to *The Letter of Aristeas*, was completed in seventy-two days. Some accounts say the translators worked with one another, sharing and comparing the work as they progressed. Other accounts say the translators were separated into different cells, and yet all the parts aligned and conformed perfectly to the Hebrew original.

THE CANON OF THE JEWISH BIBLE OR OLD TESTAMENT

There are twenty-four books in the Hebrew canon, arranged in three groupings. The first is the Torah, or Law, consisting of the first five "books of Moses":
- Genesis, Exodus, Leviticus, Numbers, and Deuteronomy

Second is the Nevi'im, or Prophets, with nineteen books and further subdivision as follows:
- Former Prophets: Joshua, Judges, Samuel, Kings
- Latter Prophets: Isaiah, Jeremiah, Ezekiel, and the Book of the Twelve (or "Minor Prophets"): Hosea, Joel, Amos, Obadiah, Jonah, Micah, Nahum, Habakkuk, Zephaniah, Haggai, Zechariah, and Malachi

Third is the Ketuvim, or Writings, which includes eleven books:

---

[33] Flavius Josephus, Antiquities of the Jews, Book XII, ii
[34] Philo of Alexandria, De Vita Moysis, II, vi

- Psalms, Proverbs, Job
- The Megillot ("Scrolls"): Song of Songs, Ruth, Lamentations, Ecclesiastes, Esther
- Daniel, Ezra & Nehemiah (as one book), Chronicles

This is the standard canon used in all printed versions of the Hebrew Bible. It is the same content as the English translations, with the exception that English Bibles separate Ezra and Nehemiah, and Samuel, Kings, and Chronicles into first and second parts.

The names of the Old Testament books as we have them in our English translations are not the same as what is in the Hebrew Bible, of course. The Hebrew books are named according to the first few words recorded in each book, or the primary subject of the book. The full listing of the books of the Bible with their Hebrew names are listed in Appendix C. Here are the Hebrew to English transliterated names of the Torah books:

- Beresheet, meaning "in the beginning" (Genesis)
- Shemot, meaning "names" (Exodus)
- Vayikra, meaning "and he called" (Leviticus)
- Bemidvar, meaning "in the desert" (Numbers)
- Devarim, meaning "words" (Deuteronomy)

So how did we end up with the English names we have had for centuries that seem so different from the Hebrew originals? The English names were ultimately derived from the Greek Septuagint translation of the Bible, along with influence from the fourth century AD Latin "Vulgate" translation. The Greek names have been in existence from the third century BC, and were ostensibly given by Jewish translators. So the source for our "odd" English titles are actually Jewish scholars!

The Septuagint's Torah or Pentateuch,[35] using English transliterations from Greek:

- Genesis (Greek for "origins")
- Exodos (Greek for "exodus")
- Leuticon (Greek for "relating to the Levites")
- Arithmoi (Greek for "numbers")
- Deuteronomion (Greek for "second law")

---

[35] Pentateuch means "five volumes" in Greek

by, Michael J. Chenevey

OLD TESTAMENT CANON AND THE APOCRYPHA (OR DEUTEROCANON)

In several places in the Scripture we read (in paraphrase), "nothing can be added to or changed" (Deut. 4:2, 12:32; Rev. 22:18f). Is the canon of the Bible closed today? The Jewish canon is typically understood to have been closed by 70 AD, before the destruction of the second temple by the Romans.[36] However, it is actually still in dispute by Christians and Jews around the world today; not the entire Old Testament, but rather certain books which were included in the Septuagint are the ones in question. These are called the Apocrypha, which means "hidden" or "obscure." Some Christians call it the deuterocanon, or "secondary" canon. These would also fit under the Hebrew designation, "Baraita," meaning outside the Mishna, which is the oral commentary or explanation of the Law.

How much of the Jewish Scriptures was translated for the Septuagint is not known. What is known is that the "full" copy in the Alexandrian library eventually contained works that were primarily written in Greek or Aramaic, and represent events in Israel's history after the fifth century BC, when the writings of the prophets were thought to have been closed.[37] In the Septuagint, we have books that most modern Protestant Christians don't know about, among them are Tobit, Judith, Bel and the Dragon, and the Maccabees. All the various groups of Roman Catholic[38] and Orthodox Christians know these, and read them as inspired Scripture. They were, after all, included in Israel's canon in the centuries before the advent of Jesus. The Jews themselves seemed to consider all the books of the Septuagint of importance, although they don't tend to write about such things as "canons" or "inspired" writings.

---

[36] It has been proposed that there was a meeting of Jewish leaders in the first century that declared the Hebrew canon closed and also expelled from the synagogue Jews who had become Christians, called the "Council of Jamnia (Or Jabneh). However, there is little to no evidence, other than that which is of the scant circumstantial variety, to support such a council in a historic sense. Some say John 9:22 references this council. See Robert C. Newman, 'The Council of Jamnia and the Old Testament Canon' (1983) for an in-depth discussion of the subject at the *Interdisciplinary Biblical Research Institute* and also http://jewishencyclopedia.com/articles/711-academies-in-palestine

[37] http://www.jewishencyclopedia.com/articles/3259-bible-canon

[38] It is of interest to note that the Roman Catholics did not emphatically declare the Apocrypha part of the divinely inspired canon until 1546, at the Council of Trent. Up until then, all Christians read these works along with the canonical books.

However, it is important to note that the "apocryphal" writings that were included in the third century BC Septuagint were included in nearly every English translation of the Bible up through the nineteenth century (typically as an appendix, at minimum). The Apocrypha was included in every major Protestant version of the English Bible from Coverdale (1535) to the Revised Standard Version (1952).[39] Yes, these books were also included in the original 1611 Authorized, or King James translation. The sixteenth century reformers Martin Luther, John Calvin, and Ulrich Zwingli also included them. So we should consider them of importance, whether or not we consider them divinely inspired.

TRANSLATIONS AND HELPFUL RESOURCES

Before we get too much further into the Old Testament, this is a good place to discuss translations for both the Old and New Testaments, and some tools we can use to

> ### Did You Know?
>
> There is no "J" in Hebrew, Aramaic, or Greek. So why does the English Bible translate proper nouns that begin with "Y" as "J"? i.e., Jesus for Yohoshua and Jacob for Yacov?
>
> "J" as an individual letter has only existed since the medieval ages. Before the "J" there was an "I" (Latin), which, in turn was a transliteration of the "Y" sound.

understand them better. Our English translations are based on something, right? The English words we read in our Bibles are not actually the original inspired words, of course. Most Christians understand this situation, and unless they are biblical scholars who understand Hebrew and Greek, they are aware they are reading a *translation*. But what does that mean? Is a translation bad? Is it to be questioned? Well, it is of course not bad. Even first century Christians primarily read translations of the Hebrew Bible in Aramaic, Syriac, and Greek, among other languages. The Bible in general and especially the most important theological concepts all believers need to know are plainly understood in any language. However, those who have read through the entire Bible notice from time to time that parts of the Scripture seem hard to understand or disjointed. Assuming the reader is not trying to read and understand an ancient version of English like the original Elizabethan King James Version (which is very difficult to understand for us modern English speakers, But then again so is

---

[39] F.F. Bruce, The Canon of Scripture, (Downer's Grove, IL: InterVarsity Press, 1988), p 114 (footnote)

Chaucer's *Canterbury Tales*, or *Beowulf*, or Shakespeare's plays), this difficulty is not the language itself but the underlying text that is the issue. Some concepts just don't come across very easily from one language and culture to another. So we do need to be aware that we will run into these challenges from time to time, and 99% of the time they do not affect our theology at all. In fact, it is likely that the situation is more like 100% of the time, since the primary disputed parts are corroborated in other more clear places. No doubt God had this translation conundrum in mind, and allowed for redundancy of His thoughts from multiple writers to make sure we understand what He wants.

There are many Christians who want to understand everything in the Bible, and are willing to slog through the tough parts by using helps. The challenging parts of Scripture do require a bit of understanding of the underlying Hebrew, Aramaic, or Greek. This is why we have "technicians of the faith" who put together resources such as the *Strong's Exhaustive Concordance*, the *Vines Expository Dictionary*, and the many devotional commentaries on the non-technical side.[40] On the scholarly side we have the *Biblia Hebraica Stuttgartensia* (the Masoretic Hebrew text), the Nestle Aland *Novum Testamentum Graece* editions of the Greek New Testament, the Brown-Driver-Briggs *Hebrew and English Lexicon*, the *Theological Dictionary of the New and Old Testaments*, and many Greek New Testament Lexicons, along with many scholarly commentaries such as the *Word Biblical Commentary* or the *New International Commentary on the Old and New Testaments*. Those who want to take the deep dive into our Bibles will enjoy each of the above resources!

MANUSCRIPT EVIDENCE

As with the concept of translations discussed above, we need a discussion about the ancient manuscripts behind our Old and New Testaments. We call "extant" those ancient manuscripts that are still available for us to put our literal or virtual[41] hands on and read original handwritten manuscripts. Today we have thousands of these

---

[40] A couple of good examples of devotional commentaries include F.B. Meyer's Bible Commentary, Matthew Henry's Complete Commentary on the Whole Bible.

[41] Virtual in the sense that quite a number of these invaluable manuscripts have been scanned and made available online for us to access without having to have scholarly credentials or travel extensively.

ancient manuscripts of both the Old and New Testaments in various conditions, languages, and levels of completeness as regards the canon (fragments to full books), that exist in many locations around the world and are typically managed by libraries, academic institutions, museums, etc.. The number of New Testament manuscripts outnumbers the Old Testament. Each manuscript is incomplete by itself, but altogether they represent the entire Bible as we know it (including the Hebrew Apocrypha). They range in age from the second century BC (Dead Sea Scrolls) until the late eighteenth century. Some of the manuscripts are lectionaries, used by the early church in worship services, some are quotations of the Bible from early church fathers (early

Photograph of Konstantin von Tischendorf (1815-1874)
Unknown -
http://www.burgmueller.com/tischendorf.html

church leadership who wrote theological treatises, sermons, commentaries, etc.), and others are rabbinic commentary and translations. Although the manuscripts are scattered all around the world, all of them have been carefully catalogued using a few systems that have evolved over the years. The most exhaustive and authoritative catalog, which now can be searched online, is managed by the Institute for New Testament Textual Research (Institut für Neutestamentliche Textforschung), abbreviated INTF at the University of Munster in Westphalia, Germany.[42] The INTF was founded by Kurt Aland, the world renowned German biblical scholar, in 1959. The Center for the Study of New Testament Manuscripts (CSNTM) at the Dallas Theological Seminary has been actively collecting digital photographs of as many ancient biblical manuscripts as possible since 2003, and has a digital manuscript catalogue system available online.[43]

Interestingly enough, the "finds" of these ancient writings actually reached a peak in the late nineteenth century. There were real "Indiana Jones" type people who, funded by governments and other organizations, traveled around the world seeking to find and collect ancient biblical manuscripts.

One such person was Constantin von Tischendorf:

> *"In 1844, he paid his first visit to the convent of*
> *Saint Catherine's Monastery, on Mount Sinai,*
> *where he found, in a trash basket, forty-four pages*
> *of what was the then oldest known copy of the*
> *Septuagint. The monks were using the trash to*
> *start fires, Tischendorf horrified, asked if he could*
> *have them. He deposited them at the University of*
> *Leipzig, under the title of the Codex Friderico-*
> *Augustanus, a name given in honour of his patron,*
> *Frederick Augustus II of Saxony, king of Saxony.*
> *The fragments were published in 1846 although he*
> *kept the place of discovery a secret"*[44]

The manuscript Tischendorf found at Saint Catherine's monastery is today called the Codex Sinaiticus,[45] a famous early, nearly complete manuscript of the Greek Septuagint from the fourth century AD.

---

[42] http://ntvmr.uni-muenster.de/home

[43] http://www.csntm.org/

[44] http://en.wikipedia.org/wiki/Constantin_von_Tischendorf

[45] http://codexsinaiticus.org/en/

OLD TESTAMENT MANUSCRIPTS

Approximately 3,375 Hebrew manuscripts exist today.[46]   The largest single collection of over 2,000 are in the Imperial Library in St. Petersburg, Russia. We have approximately 630 Greek manuscripts[47] and approximately 250 Syriac manuscripts.[48]

MASORETES (HEBREW)

The earliest extant Hebrew manuscripts date from the ninth century AD and were a product of a group of Jewish scholars called the Masoretes. Masorete comes from the Hebrew word Masorah, meaning "tradition." The Masorete scholars, circa sixth to tenth century AD, lived primarily in Israel, in Jerusalem and Tiberias, but also in Babylonia (modern Iraq) and were dedicated to keeping the Jewish Scriptures as consistent as possible. Their text, called the "Masoretic Text," is often referred to as the MT. Have you read the Introduction to your Bible lately? It will mention the MT as a source for the Old Testament.   This text was an effort to stabilize the pronunciation of Hebrew, as the Masoretes understood it. As mentioned earlier, Hebrew is a consonantal language. The Masoretes created a system of dots and dashes, placed around the consonants so as not to alter the text, in order to represent vowels. Their effort was relatively late; however, it is the only representation of

---

[46] http://www.newadvent.org/cathen/09627a.htm

[47] http://www.newadvent.org/cathen/09627a.htm

[48] http://www.newadvent.org/cathen/09627a.htm

A page from the Masoretic text (Aleppo Codex).
Shlomo ben Buya'a - http://www.aleppocodex.org Photograph by Ardon Bar Hama. (C) 2007 The Yad Yitzhak Ben Zvi Institute.

biblical Hebrew pronunciation we have today. Unfortunately, although the Masoretes' modifications allow us to read the text, we now know they made mistakes. Based upon other Old Testament translations (e.g., the Septuagint) and non-biblical evidence such as the Canaanite Tel-Amarna letters,[49] it is obvious that the Masoretic Text deviates from the original biblical language at many points.| The printed editions of the Masoretic text date back to 1488, with the first entire Old Testament in print.[50] The Hebrew texts from the early age of printing were based upon what is called the *textus receptus* or "received text." However, the *textus receptus* was based on relatively late manuscript evidence from the fourteenth and fifteenth centuries. This tradition of using the late manuscripts was followed even into the twentieth century. The twentieth century editions include Ginsberg's 1926 version and Rudolf Kittle's *Biblia Hebraica* (or BHK), known in three editions (1906, 1909, 1937). The 1937 edition of Kittle's *Biblia Hebraica* (BH³) broke with the *textus receptus*, instead utilizing manuscripts three to four centuries older than the previous editions.[51] The text of the BH³ was derived directly from the Leningrad Codex (a manuscript referred to as B 19^A (L), located today in the Public Library of St. Petersburg, Russia). This Codex is the earliest complete Masoretic manuscript in existence, dating from 1008 or 1009 AD.[52] The latest version of Kittle's work, the *Biblia Hebraica Stuttgartensia* (1967), incorporates more textual information than its predecessors.

The Leningrad Codex, the basis for all modern Hebrew editions, just happens to be the only complete manuscript to have survived the medieval ages. Its survival does not necessitate its authority, nor does it necessarily corroborate with the many copies in existence prior to its emergence. Simply put, it is not the only authoritative version of the Hebrew text in existence. The *Biblia Hebraica* versions provide alternative readings in footnote form, representing many other ancient manuscripts, ". . . each of which was considered both authoritative and 'standard' by some."[53] Variants are not irregularities, but viable alternative readings with just as much authority as the Leningrad Codex.

---

[49] William Sanford LaSor, Old Testament Survey, (Grand Rapids, MI: Eerdmans, 1996), p. 28.

[50] Otto Eissfeldt, The Old Testament, An Introduction, (New York: Harper and Row, 1965), p. 691.

[51] Eissfeldt, p. 691.

[52] The Leningrad Codex, or Leningradensis, is based upon a mid-tenth century (930 AD) manuscript by Aaron ben Moshe ben Asher (now located in Jerusalem, Israel) called the Aleppo Codex. Several older Hebrew manuscripts exist, but none are complete. The oldest Hebrew manuscript, a Cairo copy of the prophets, dates from 895 AD.

[53] Douglas Stuart, Old Testament Exegesis, (Philadelphia: The Westminster Press, 1980), p. 84.

by, Michael J. Chenevey

THE SEPTUAGINT (GREEK) MANUSCRIPTS

The earliest manuscripts we have for the Septuagint date from the fourth century AD (i.e., Codex Sinaiticus, as mentioned earlier) to the ninth century AD. There are three families of Septuagint manuscripts: 1. Hexaplaric, from early church father

Part of the Book of Esther from the Codex Sinaiticus. Image is public domain.

Origen, 2. Hesychian, from the Alexandrian region of Egypt, and 3. Lucianic, from the Antiochian region of the Middle East.

There are approximately 630 extant manuscripts of the Greek Septuagint: 16 fragments on papyrus (4th to 7th c AD), over 300 minuscules[54] on vellum (unclassified), 311 uncials[55] on vellum (4th to 9th c AD), and a few others.

The earliest extant copies of the complete Septuagint (or as we explained earlier, the LXX) date from the third and fourth centuries AD,[56] and even these represent centuries of copying. However, we know that the Septuagint originally dates from the third or second century BC. Septuagint manuscripts were not found at Qumran.[57] However, manuscripts of certain Old Testament books written in Greek were found at Qumran, providing us with more evidence concerning the Greek translations of the Old Testament prior to the first century AD.

> **Did You Know?**
>
> Some books of the Bible were written in acrostic style, for instance, Lamentations and Psalm 119. In each section, each line started with a different Hebrew letter. The acrostics are lost in our translations.

It is interesting that, despite the existence of older Greek manuscripts of the Old Testament (third century), many prefer to work Old Testament translation primarily from the much younger (eleventh century) Hebrew Masoretic Text (MT). This brings up another interesting matter. The Septuagint represents an important canon of Scripture, known and obviously cherished even by the New Testament writers. Yet it is still a *translation* from an earlier Hebrew version. How can a translation be very accurate? Actually, the Septuagint may be more accurate than one would think. One of the great advantages of the Greek manuscripts lies in the language itself. The ancient Greek language contained vowels, while the ancient Hebrew language did not. Hebrew is a consonantal language, and as such, could only have been understood by the people by whom and for whom it was written. We really do not know for certain how the Hebrew language was pronounced, say, at the time of Christ, much less hundreds of years prior to the New Testament era. Thus, the Greek translation may actually be a more

---

[54] "Minuscules" refers to Greek manuscripts that are later (from approximately 10th c AD), which have a more mature form and structure than the earlier Uncials (see next note).

[55] "Uncials" are the earliest Greek text form. They typically have large lettering (not upper and lower case, but their own form of Greek letters), with no word separation, no sentence markings, no periods or paragraphs. The words all run together on each sheet.

[56] James C. Vanderkam, The Dead Sea Scrolls Today, (Grand Rapids: William B. Eerdmans Publishing Company, 1994), p. 124.

[57] We will explain more about Qumran under the Dead Sea Scrolls (DSS) section. Qumran refers to the locale for the community that left us the DSS.

accurate representation of the ancient pre-AD Hebrew language than our extant Hebrew manuscripts. One Old Testament exegete states,

> "... the Septuagint ... is just as reliable and accurate a witness to the original wording of the [Old Testament] (the "autographs") as the [Masoretic Text] is. In many sections of the OT it is more reliable than the MT; in others less. Largely because the Greek language uses vowels and Hebrew does not, the LXX wordings were less ambiguous and the LXX less likely to be marred by textual corruptions than the Hebrew ... When you undertake textual criticism ... you should probably place the LXX side by side with the MT and treat them as equals."[58]

The Septuagint is a reliable witness, and it is also appropriate to acknowledge the fact that the Septuagint has been copied many times, and many Greek manuscripts exist. The many extant copies of the Septuagint have required the use of "critical" texts; compilations that include the primary variants (only from the Septuagint) in footnote form along with the main text. Thus, we can view all the primary differences between the Septuagint manuscripts in one volume.

---

[58] Douglas Stuart, Old Testament Exegesis, (Philadelphia: The Westminster Press, 1980), p. 91.

THE PESHITTA (SYRIAC) MANUSCRIPTS

Syriac, an early variant of Aramaic, appeared in the first century AD. It was spoken in the Fertile Crescent region and was a major literary language for over seven hundred years.[59] Syriac was one of the primary languages used by the early Christians, in addition to Latin and Greek.[60] The early Christian Bible in Syriac was known as the Peshitta. The Peshitta was likely first translated by Jews around the first or second century AD, and contained the Old Testament translated from Hebrew independent of the Septuagint. The New Testament, most likely translated from Greek originals, was added sometime before the end of the second century AD.

What is very important to understand is the role of the Peshitta in spreading Christianity in the East. In the time subsequent to the second century AD, a Syriac-based culture spread across the Asian continent. This allowed Christianity to spread into Mongolia and India ("St Thomas Christians"), and remnants of early Christianity have been found as far East as China (as early as 640 AD, according to the

Peshitta Text of Exodus 13:14-16. Plate XIII. The S.S. Teacher's Edition: The Holy Bible. New York: Henry Frowde, Publisher to the University of Oxford, 1896.

---

[59] Klaus Beyer, The Aramaic Language: its distribution and subdivisions. John F. Healey (trans.), (Göttingen: Vandenhoeck und Ruprecht, 1986), p. 44.

[60] Robert Louis Wilken, The First Thousand Years: A Global History of Christianity, (New Haven and London: Yale University Press, 2013), p. 26.

Nestorian Stele[61]) and Japan (as early as the fifth century AD, according to the remnants found at the Uzumasa-dera temple[62]). Christianity was in Japan well before Buddhism.

The earliest extant copies of the Peshitta date from the 5th century AD, for both the Old and New Testaments. Approximately 250 manuscripts of the Old Testament Peshitta have been catalogued, dating between the 5th and 12th centuries AD. Approximately 40 New Testament manuscripts exist, from the 5th to the 10 centuries AD.[63] An interesting feature of the Peshitta's New Testament is that it excludes 2 Peter, 2 John, 3 John, Jude, and Revelation.

DEAD SEA SCROLLS

In early 1947, a young Bedouin shepherd of the Ta'amireh tribe named Jum'a Muhammad Khalil[64] tossed a rock into a cave. The rock did not thud, as he expected,

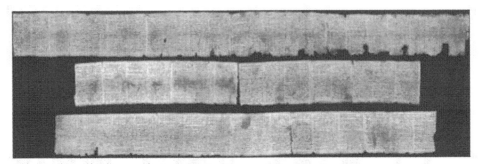

The Isaiah Scroll. Photographs by Ardon Bar Hama, website of the Israel Museum, Jerusalem

---

[61] Michael Keevak, The Story of a Stele: China's Nestorian Monument and Its Reception in the West, 1625–1916, (Hong Kong: Hong Kong University Press, 2008).

[62] http://www.japantimes.co.jp/life/2001/07/24/travel/religious-sites-relics-indicate-christ-beat-buddha-to-japan-2/#.V4rKIqK1WIo

[63] Andreas Juckel, A Guide to Manuscripts of the Peshitta New Testament, Hugoye Journal of Syriac Studies, (The Syriac Institute and Gorgias Press, 2012).

[64] James C. Vanderkam, The Dead Sea Scrolls Today, (Grand Rapids: William B. Eerdmans Publishing Company, 1994), p. 3.

but crashed into what would turn out to be the greatest archaeological discovery of modern times, the Dead Sea Scrolls (DSS). The region known as Qumran, located only a half-mile from the northwest shore of the Dead Sea was thoroughly excavated for more evidence over a period of several decades, ultimately bringing to light a treasure trove of over 900 manuscripts represented in thousands of fragments and larger parchments. Two hundred of the scrolls contained biblical compositions now known to have been written between the third century BC and first century AD.[65] The scrolls and fragments, preserved primarily on sheep and goat skins, were written in Hebrew, Greek, Aramaic, and Nabatean.

The consensus today is that the material found at Qumran represents the efforts of a group of monastic-like Jews called the Essenes. The excavations at Qumran revealed an extensive community that was occupied from as early as the eighth and seventh centuries BC until around 68 AD.[66] The Qumran community was very careful to preserve their Scriptures, along with many other documents representing their sect. This fact is proved by the remarkable similarity between later Old Testament manuscripts and the Essene copies.

The Qumran discoveries include various manuscripts, categorized as biblical (Hebrew manuscripts, Targums, tefillin, and mezuzot[67]), apocryphal (and pseudo-epigraphical[68]), commentary on biblical material and other themes, paraphrases, legal material, worship writings, eschatological works, wisdom texts, and documentary texts. Our focus is the biblical and apocryphal material.

The following apocryphal and pseudo-epigraphical material has been found at Qumran: Apocryphal: Tobit, Sirach, Letter of Jeremiah, and Psalm 151; pseudo-epigraphical: Enoch, Jubilees, and Testaments of the Twelve Patriarchs. More pseudo-epigrapha were found at Qumran, but these were previously unknown.

The Qumran discoveries are extraordinary in that they are biblical manuscripts preserved from the third through the first centuries BC. The most recent extant Old Testament manuscripts prior to the Qumran finds were from the third century AD!

---

[65] George Braziller, Scrolls from the Dead Sea, (New York: George Braziller, Inc., 1993), p. 26.

[66] Vanderkam, p. 13-14.

[67] Tefillin and mezuzot are small parchments containing passages of Scripture. Tefillin were used for phylacteries, and mezuzot for doorposts of homes (See Deut. 6:8-9). Targums are Aramaic interpretations of Scripture developed by Rabbis when Hebrew ceased to be the primary language of the Jews.

[68] Pseudo-epigrapha are those works that were produced under an assumed name (e.g., the book of Enoch – this text dates from the inter-testamental period, but was supposedly written by the biblical Enoch from Gen. 5:21-24).

The biblical material found at Qumran is summarized in the following table.[69]

Name	Number of Copies	Name	Number of Copies
Genesis	15	Psalms	36
Exodus	17	Proverbs	2
Leviticus	13	Job	4
Numbers	8	Song of Solomon	4
Deuteronomy	29	Ruth	4
Joshua	2	Lamentations	4
Judges	3	Ecclesiastes	3
1–2 Samuel	4	Esther	0
1–2 Kings	3	Daniel	8
Isaiah	21	Ezra	1
Jeremiah	6	Nehemiah	0
Ezekiel	6	1–2 Chronicles	1
The Twelve (Minor prophets)	8		

---

[69] Vanderkam, p. 30.

CHAPTER 4
THE NEW TESTAMENT

by, Michael J. Chenevey

INTRODUCTION

It is important to note that the "New Covenant" (this term is interchangeable with "New Testament") had been promised in the Old Testament (Jeremiah 31:31-34). The New Covenant was not only a promise fulfilled, but an understanding, an interpretation, or a theology of the Old Testament. One cannot stand without the other. When the risen Jesus talked with Cleopas and the other disciple on the road to Emmaus in Luke 24, he told them about himself from the Scriptures, what we call the Old Testament.[70] All of the teachings and ministry justifications given by Jesus, John the Baptist, and the apostles used the Old Testament. The Gospel that was preached by Jesus and His disciples was the Gospel of the Old Testament. The Jewish Bible was the Bible of the earliest Christian church. We must not lose sight of these facts and rely completely on the New Testament for our understanding of God's perspective and

> ### **Did You Know?**
>
> In the earliest handwritten Greek manuscripts, all text ran together with no separation of words or thoughts.

what He wants from us. Context is extremely important, and we must understand that the New Testament books were written by Jews who lived predominately in a Jewish culture.[71] It is clear in reading the New Testament in Greek that the words were not written by Greek cultured people. The New Testament authors (except Luke) use the typical structure and vocabulary of Hebrew writers. When studying and seeking to understand the New Testament, the inquirer must take the Hebrew or Jewish culture into account, for it is the culture of the New Testament.

Some may bring in the Apostle Paul and make the case that he was writing to non-Jews. In fact, in Acts, it is clear that even though he was called to reach the gentiles, early in his ministry he tried reaching out to the Jews first by arguing in the synagogues and marketplaces. But he decided he would change tactics because of their stubbornness and go only to the gentiles. Yet, as we read his epistles to gentile churches (e.g., Romans is a great example) where he makes the case for the Gospel of the Messiah Jesus, he uses a fully Jewish context for doing so. He constantly quotes

---

[70] Luke 24:27

[71] Perhaps the writings of Luke (Gospel of Luke and Acts of the Apostles) represent the only non-Jewish author in the New Testament. But Luke, although he may have been a gentile convert, was heavily influenced in thought by the Jewish Apostle Paul.

the Old Testament in making his case. It is clear he is working to graft gentile branches into the Jewish tree and root structure of the Hebrew Scriptures.

LANGUAGE OF THE NEW TESTAMENT

The New Testament was written in Koine ("common"), or Alexandrian Greek. This is significant because this variant of Greek is not the classical or literary language used by philosophers and playwrights at the height of the classical period, circa 600 BC and later which is called Attic Greek (centered geographically around Athens), but Koine was the common or street language used in everyday interlocution and commerce around the known world, and had many local variants. Koine was also the variant of Greek used for the Septuagint.

Greek culture and language had been brought to the greater Mediterranean and Middle East regions by Alexander the Great's conquests in the fourth century BC. As he advanced throughout Europe, the Middle East, Northern Africa, Asia, and even into India, the Greek culture, language and characteristics followed and persisted for hundreds of years afterwards, even to today in some places. This Greek cultural change is referred to as "Hellenization." Hellenization is an important concept in the early church, as reported in the Acts of the Apostles and Pauls' writings. It affected the Jews in Jerusalem and the new Christian community deeply.[72]

THE NEW TESTAMENT CANON

The collection of books (canon) we now call the New Testament was certainly in place sometime before 190 AD. In 180 AD church father Irenaeus, Bishop of Lyons, recorded the four Gospels together for the first time.[73] The first albeit incomplete list of canonical books shows up in what is called the Muratorian Fragment, or Muratorian Canon, dated to around 190 AD. This 85-line Latin "fragment" was copied into a later work written in the seventh century by an unknown author. The later work ended up

---

[72] Acts 6:1 refers to two different groups of Jewish believers; those who retained the Hebrew culture as primary, and those who had been Hellenized (and spoke Greek primarily).

[73] Irenaeus, Against Heresies, Book III.

in the library of the Bobbio Abbey in Italy, then was transferred to the Ambrosian Library in Milan, where it was re-discovered by Ludovico Antonio Muratori (1672-1750)[74] who published it in 1740. The Muratorian fragment lists the following books:

The Gospels of Luke and John, Acts of the Apostles, Romans, 1 and 2 Corinthians, Galatians, Ephesians, Philippians, Colossians, 1 and 2 Thessalonians, 1 and 2 Timothy, Titus, Philemon, 1 and 2 John (or possibly 3 John; it is not clear), Jude, Revelation. Missing are the first two Gospels (the fragment is incomplete at the beginning): Matthew and Mark, along with Hebrews, James, 1 and 2 Peter and 3 John (or 2 John, it is not clear).

The famous Council of Nicea (325 AD), called by the Roman Emperor Constantine to settle disputes among the church leadership, was the first ecumenical council for the entire Christian church. Bishop Athanasius records that either 300 or more precisely 318 leaders were present.[75] These leaders had copies of what we call the New Testament, and it is very likely that these copies reflect the same 27-book canon we have today.[76] No historian records anything about canonical discussions at the council, but in 330 AD, Constantine ordered fifty copies of the complete Christian Bible, in Greek, from Eusebius Pamphilus of Caesarea.[77]

The official canon as we have them today, 27 books, was established for certain by 367 AD. In his Thirty-ninth Festal Letter, Athanasius, Bishop of Alexandria writes:[78]

> *"Again it is not tedious to speak of the [books] of the New Testament. These are, the four Gospels, according to Matthew, Mark, Luke, and John. Afterwards, the Acts of the Apostles and Epistles (called Catholic), seven, viz. of James, one; of Peter, two; of John, three; after these, one of Jude. In addition, there are fourteen Epistles of Paul,*

---

[74] Barbara Aland and Kurt Aland, The Text of the New Testament: An Introduction to the Critical Editions and to the Theory and Practice of Modern Textual Criticism, (Grand Rapids: E. J. Brill, 1987), p. 48.

[75] http://www.newadvent.org/cathen/11044a.htm

[76] F.F. Bruce, The Canon of Scripture, (Downer's Grove: InterVarsity Press, 1988), P.204

[77] Philip Schaff and Henry Wace Eds., Nicene and Post-Nicene Fathers, Second Series, Vol. 1., (Buffalo, NY: Christian Literature Publishing Co., 1892.)

[78] F.F. Bruce, P.209.

written in this order. The first, to the Romans; then two to the Corinthians; after these, to the Galatians; next, to the Ephesians; then to the Philippians; then to the Colossians; after these, two to the Thessalonians, and that to the Hebrews; and again, two to Timothy; one to Titus; and lastly, that to Philemon. And besides, the Revelation of John. These are fountains of salvation, that they who thirst may be satisfied with the living words they contain. In these alone is proclaimed the doctrine of godliness. Let no man add to these, neither let him take ought from these. For concerning these the Lord put to shame the Sadducees, and said, 'You err, not knowing the Scriptures.' And He reproved the Jews, saying, 'Search the Scriptures, for these are they that testify of Me.' But for greater exactness I add this also, writing of necessity; that there are other books besides these not indeed included in the Canon, but appointed by the Fathers to be read by those who newly join us, and who wish for instruction in the word of godliness. The Wisdom of Solomon, and the Wisdom of Sirach, and Esther, and Judith, and Tobit, and that which is called the Teaching of the Apostles, and the Shepherd. But the former, my brethren, are included in the Canon, the latter being [merely] read; nor is there in any place a mention of apocryphal writings. But they are an invention of heretics, who write them when they choose, bestowing upon them their approbation, and assigning to them a date, that so, using them as ancient writings, they may find occasion to lead astray the simple."[79]

Bishop Athanasius mentions the non-canonical Apocryphal books which were included in the Septuagint, then also references two later non-canonical works from the late first or early second century AD, the Teaching of the Apostles, also known as the Didache and the Shepherd of Hermas, also called the Pastor of Hermas. Both of these works are considered important reading for Christians.

DIVISIONS OF THE NEW TESTAMENT

The New Testament is divided into several sections, as follows:
- Gospels: Matthew, Mark, Luke, John. The first three Gospels, which are closer in age and content, are referred to as the "Synoptic" Gospels. The Gospel of John was written later, toward the end of the first century and generally contains sections that are not found in the other three.
- Pauline Epistles: Romans, 1 and 2 Corinthians, Galatians, Ephesians, Philippians, Colossians, Thessalonians, Philemon
- Pastoral Epistles: Titus, Timothy
- General or "Catholic" Epistles: James, 1 and 2 Peter, 1, 2, and 3 John, Jude
- Acts of the Apostles
- Hebrews
- Revelation

Appendix D lists the entire canon with details about each book, such as author, date, and other important information.

NEW TESTAMENT APOCRYPHA

Typically when Christians refer to "the Apocrypha" they are thinking about the Old Testament books that were included in the Greek Septuagint, and which many

---

[79] Philip Schaff and Henry Wace Eds., Nicene and Post-Nicene Fathers, Second Series, Vol. 4., (Buffalo, NY: Christian Literature Publishing Co., 1892.) The quotation from Athanasius' letter can be found online at: http://www.newadvent.org/fathers/2806039.htm

Christians include in their inspired canon. However, a number of apocryphal works are associated with the early church. Some of these non-canonical works are fairly orthodox and have been promoted by such leaders as St. Athanasius, while many others are spurious, written by those who were considered heretics and schismatics, who ended up separated from the main body of believers. The full listing of the Apocryphal works, both useful and spurious, is presented in Appendix E. Note that the Christian apocryphal works far outnumber the Jewish ones, and many of them are spurious.

> **Did You Know?**
>
> In 1205, Archbishop Stephen Langton and Cardinal Hugo de Sancto Caro developed the first systematic division of the Bible (Old and New Testaments) into chapters for the Latin Vulgate.

Two works that are worth mentioning are the Didache and Shepherd of Hermas. Both works were considered part of the canonical New Testament by some church fathers, and not by others.

The Didache (Greek for "teaching"), or Teaching of the Apostles dates to the late first century or early second century AD. The Didache consists of three parts. The first part is the "Two Ways": the Way of Life (love God and love our neighbor) and the Way of Death (sins). The second part is about baptism, fasting, and Holy Communion. The third part is about ministry.

Some notable parts of the Teachings:

- Baptism is to be done in living water, in the name of the Father, and of the Son, and of the Holy Spirit. Also, the person to be baptized and the baptizer should each fast for one or two days prior to the event.
- Fasts should be on Wednesday and Friday, not on Monday or Thursday, as the Jews do.
- Christians should pray the Lord's Prayer three times daily.
- Every Apostle is to be received as the Lord, and he may stay one or two days. If he stays three days, he is a false prophet. Also, if he asks for money, he is a false prophet.
- Firstfruits (tithes) are to be given to the prophets, for they are the "high priests," but if we have no prophets, give the firstfruits to the poor.

The Shepherd of Hermas, or the "Shepherd" was bound with the other New Testament books in the Codex Sinaiticus. It contains five visions, twelve moral mandates, and ten parables; most in allegory and focusing on calling the church to be faithful and repent of sins.

Some notable parts of the Shepherd:[80]

- ". . . fear not the devil; for, fearing the Lord, you will have dominion over the devil, for there is no power in him. But he in whom there is no power ought on no account to be an object of fear; but He in whom there is glorious power is truly to be feared" (Mandate 7).

> ## Did You Know?
>
> In 1551, Robert Estienne (a Protestant) developed verse numbering for his Greek New Testament. Estienne's system is now used in nearly all modern Bibles. The Geneva Bible was the first full Bible to use this system, in 1560.

- "Put away doubting from you and do not hesitate to ask of the Lord, saying to yourself, 'How can I ask of the Lord and receive from Him, seeing I have sinned so much against Him? 'Do not thus reason with yourself, but with all your heart turn to the Lord and ask of Him without doubting, and you will know the multitude of His tender mercies; that He will never leave you, but fulfil the request of your soul" (Mandate 9).

- ". . . if you return to the Lord with all your heart, and practice righteousness the rest of your days, and serve Him according to His will, He will heal your former sins, and you will have power to hold sway over the works of the devil. But as to the threats of the devil, fear them not at all, for he is powerless as the sinews of a dead man" (Mandate 12, Chapter 6).

MANUSCRIPT EVIDENCE

The number of New Testament manuscripts we have today is far more than those of the Old Testament. What is astounding is, prior to 1870 and the discoveries made by collectors such as Constantin von Tischendorf, we only knew of about 1,000 ancient (pre-12th century AD) Greek manuscripts. Today we have approximately 5,800 extant ancient Greek manuscripts,[81] as well as 10,000 Latin manuscripts and over 9,300 manuscripts in other ancient languages including Syriac, Slavic, Gothic, Ethiopic,

---

[80] Quotations are from Philip Schaff and Henry Wace Eds., Ante-Nicene Fathers, Second Series, (Buffalo, NY: Christian Literature Publishing Co., 1892.)

[81] Norman Geisler and Peter Bocchino, Unshakeable Foundations, (Minneapolis, MN: Bethany House Publishers, 2001) p. 256. The *Liste Handschriften*, as the INTF calls its authoritative list of New Testament manuscripts, lists 5,789 manuscripts as of October, 2016.

Coptic, and Armenian. The majority of the non-Greek manuscripts are later than tenth century AD.

A few previously undiscovered, or sometimes unrecorded, biblical manuscripts turn up regularly every year, especially those of the New Testament. This leads to additional questions, of course. Some anticipated questions have been addressed in Chapter Three, under Manuscript Evidence, such as who manages the number and importance of ancient biblical manuscripts and where are they located after they have been found. It is important to keep in mind that the vast majority of these newly discovered manuscripts are relatively late, after the tenth century AD. Consider that the Bible's proliferation has increased dramatically over the ages, and continues to do so today, at the instigation of Christians who seek to get the Bible in the hands of as many people as possible. As far as where these manuscripts come from, they may have been hidden away in churches, rediscovered in libraries, or found through archaeological efforts.

Sometimes changes in political regimes allow access to previously unresearched manuscripts, such as what happened in Albania in July, 2007. For decades, scholars had understood there were thirty Greek New Testament manuscripts in the country of Albania. However, because of the inaccessibility of the manuscripts due to government control, the manuscripts' content was not known, or known accurately. In 2007, a group from the Center for the Study of New Testament Manuscripts (CSNTM) at Dallas Theological Seminary was able to gain access to the Albanian National Archives and found forty-seven manuscripts, not thirty![82]

The discovery of pre-eleventh century biblical manuscripts is rare, and generally celebrated in the public news when it does happen (typically well after they are announced and studied in academic circles and publications).

TEXT TYPES AND CATEGORIES

Given the enormous task of managing and understanding ancient biblical manuscripts, scholars have developed various classification schemes. The classifications have been developed based on the manuscript age (using, among other methods, carbon-14 dating), types of media, binding, and ink used, handwriting style, letter type (i.e., uncial or minuscule), language, vocabulary, and other factors. These factors help to determine, within some range of error, how scholars determine their

---

[82]https://bible.org/article/greek-new-testament-manuscripts-discovered-albania

provenance (original source, no matter where they are ultimately discovered geographically). We will introduce the most well respected classifications below. Generally, New Testament manuscripts have been classified into "text types" and, alternatively, "categories."

There are three text types that have been recognized:

1. **Alexandrian:** The earliest and best preserved manuscripts from the second to the fourth centuries AD. Examples include Codex Sinaiticus and Codex Vaticanus. These manuscripts used papyrus media and originated around Alexandria, Egypt.

2. **Western (also known as Caesarean):** The Western text type dates from the third to the ninth centuries, and was copied and used by a wide range of churches in the west (from North Africa to Italy to Gaul). Codex Bezae is an example. These are written in Greek and Latin, but less quality controlled than the Alexandrian type.

3. **Byzantine (also called the Majority Text):** The vast majority (approximately 95%) of known manuscripts are of the Byzantine text type. These manuscripts date from the fifth century to the sixteenth century. The Byzantine text is called thus because of its popularity in Constantinople, the capital of the Byzantine empire, around the fifth century. It is known to contain harmonizations, paraphrasing, and some significant additions. It has its challenges, and underlies the Textus Receptus ("Received Text") behind many reformation era texts and translations, including the 1611 Authorized or King James translation.

In the early 1980's Kurt and Barbara Aland sought to improve the "text type" approach and introduced five categories of manuscripts based on unique characteristics derived from one thousand passages where the Byzantine and non-Byzantine texts differ the greatest.[83] The five categories range from the Alexandrian type to the Byzantine type, with three categories in between.

Category I: Alexandrian

The Alexandrian category includes the earliest manuscripts, primarily the papyrus-based uncials. Many scholars believe this type reflects closest the "Autographs" or original texts, since they are the oldest manuscripts we have. Thus, they are used to help with textual problems in other texts.

Category II: Egyptian

---

[83] Barbara Aland and Kurt Aland, The Text of the New Testament: An Introduction to the Critical Editions and to the Theory and Practice of Modern Textual Criticism, (Grand Rapids: E. J. Brill, 1987).

Manuscripts in the Egyptian category are similar to the Alexandrian category, however, they tend to contain issues related to quality control.

Category III: Eclectic

Manuscripts in the Eclectic category contain unique independent readings and are separated by their unique mixed or eclectic character.

Category IV: Western

The Western category includes manuscripts that follow the Codex Bezae, known as the Western texts.

Category V: Byzantine

The Byzantine category includes the majority of manuscripts in existence; a wide range of copies that exhibit significant paraphrasing and additions.

SUMMARY OF TEXTUAL IMPORTANCE

The different classifications are most important to Christians because they describe the material used by translators when developing English Bibles. Each of the many English Bible translations we have is based on either a selection of manuscripts or a specific type. See Appendix F for a list of English translations from the late seventh century AD to 2010.

Here are some examples of English translations and their associated classification:

Table 4.1. A short comparison of English Bible translations based on their underlying text types.

New International Version (NIV), American Standard Version (ASV), New American Standard Version (NASV), Douay, Revised Standard Version (RSV), New Revised Standard Version (NRSV), English Standard Version (ESV)	Primarily Alexandrian Text Type/Category I
King James Version (KJV), New King James Version (NKJV)	Byzantine Text Type/Category V

CHAPTER 5
INERRANCY AND BIBLICAL TEXTUAL CRITICISM

BIBLICAL INERRANCY

The forthcoming discussion regarding biblical textual criticism and variants leads to an obvious question: Does the Bible contain "errors," or more to the point, is the Bible inerrant? What do people mean when they say the Bible is "inerrant"? Is the entire Bible, every verse, always true? The concept of biblical inerrancy does not, as commonly thought, have to do with the precision with which events are recorded, or even challenges with copyist errors, which do not predominantly affect doctrine. It has to do with the truthfulness of what is written. Systematic Theologian Wayne Grudem defines inerrancy, "*Scripture in the original manuscripts does not affirm anything that is contrary to fact.*"[84] Scripture itself tells us that God cannot lie (Titus 1:2); thus, as God's words, Scripture cannot lie.

How precise must a statement be to be true? For instance, the biblical writers speak of the sun rising (e.g., Genesis 19:23; 32:31; Mark 16:2). From a scientific standpoint, this is incorrect. The sun does not rise; the earth rotates. Yet, the statement is still true from the author's point of view. Language can make vague or imprecise statements without being untrue. Again, the statement, "I went to college in Ohio" is a true statement, but it is vague and imprecise; it does not say in which city the college is located or when matriculation took place.

Several major challenges would arise if we were to deny biblical inerrancy. If God's word is not truthful, may we imitate God and intentionally lie in small affairs also? Can we really trust God with anything he says in Scripture? Or, if the Bible is wrong in minor details, then it can be wrong in its doctrines as well. If we stand in judgment upon the Bible, and assume from our limited perspective that Scripture is wrong (that is, without God's perspective), then we essentially make our minds higher than Scripture.

---

[84] Wayne Grudem, Systematic Theology, An Introduction to Biblical Doctrine, (Grand Rapids: Zondervan, 1994). P.90

by, Michael J. Chenevey

INTRODUCTION TO TEXTUAL CRITICISM

How do we know if what we have in our Bibles corresponds to that which was originally written, what scholars call the "autographs"? Some may ask why this is even an issue. We have copies of the original texts, so why don't we just translate these? It is not that straightforward. We have thousands of ancient copies of the Old and New Testaments that exist in many languages including Hebrew, Greek, Aramaic, Syriac, Latin, Coptic, and Ethiopic, and these range in age from about 250 BC to the sixteenth century Reformation era. Many of the Old Testament manuscripts, for instance, are translations from the Greek Septuagint, some are copies of the Hebrew original (e.g., the Samaritan Pentateuch and the Dead Sea Scrolls), and some are translations of Hebrew originals (e.g., the Targums, Syriac, and Latin versions). As to the New Testament, the original writings were Greek and Hebrew or Aramaic,[85] and early on translated into a number of languages corresponding to people groups ranging from what is modern Europe and North Africa to the peoples of the East, as far as China and possibly Japan.[86] Compounding the problem of so many texts of the Old and New Testaments is the textual variants found among so many manuscripts. How do scholars grapple with these seemingly overwhelming challenges? They utilize the procedures of what is known as the discipline of textual criticism. This chapter includes an overview of textual criticism. Appendix H is a fuller and more technical article on textual criticism for those who want more details on the processes, historical methods, and prominent textual critics.

Textual criticism is known as a "lower" criticism, as opposed to the so-called "higher" criticisms that often employ very subjective methodologies. It is called lower because textual critics deal with objective data – actual manuscripts and their differences. Textual critics seek to discern the original text among the numerous variants. The description, "numerous variants" seems overwhelming, but it is relative in the sense that, although thousands of variations exist among the various biblical manuscripts, the majority of differences are of no consequence to translation and,

---

[85] The early church father Papias of Hieropolis (125-150 AD) explained that, "Matthew compiled the sayings [of the Lord] in the Aramaic language, and everyone translated them as well as he could." (Explanation of the Sayings of the Lord [cited by Eusebius in History of the Church 3:39]). In 180 AD, Irenaeus of Lyons wrote, "Matthew also issued a written Gospel among the Hebrews in their own dialect." (Against Heresies 3:1:1).

[86] See Chapter 3 for references explaining the expansion of Christianity in Eastern Syriac-speaking regions.

more importantly, interpretation and doctrine (e.g., certain manuscripts may leave out definite articles or skip words which appear in similar manuscripts).

How does one "do" textual criticism? How do we really know which variant is correct and which is not? The answer is, ultimately we do not know for certain. Every textual critic must introduce subjective analysis at some point in his or her methodology. We must constantly keep in mind that the original manuscripts (the autographs) do not exist anymore. All we have today are copies; thus, by the nature of the copying process over thousands of years, every manuscript we study contains flaws. Our job is to minimize these flaws through certain techniques for determining the best reading. We will discuss the guidelines for doing textual criticism shortly.

VARIANTS: MISTAKES AND CORRUPTIONS

What is a variant? These are any discrepancies in the words used among the many thousands of handwritten and printed manuscripts we have extant for both the Old and New Testaments in a number of languages, [87] against a standard text.[88] The vast majority of the differences are unintentional scribal errors, as described below, that do not affect meaning and are therefore inconsequential. Some are more intentional, for instance where sections of text have been added by copyists to improve the text.

There are two primary types of variants:
- **Unintentional Variants**, due to natural error:
    - Dittography: Repetition of a letter, word, or phrase
    - Homoioteleuton: Omission of a letter, word, or phrase
    - Haplography: Omission of a word repeated in the text
    - Itacism: Copyist mistake of spelling or grammar
    - Orthographic: Differences in spelling, word breaks, emphasis, or punctuation
- **Intentional Variants**, due to a desire for improvement of the text:
    - Marginal notes
    - Added traditional readings
    - Grammatical improvements

---

[87] Besides Greek, the translations used for textual variant counts include Latin, Coptic, Syriac, Georgian, Armenian, Ethiopic and others.

[88] Today a "standard text" might be the 28th edition of the Nestle-Aland (NA) New Testament in Greek, which is the same as the United Bible Society (UBS) 5th edition.

- Harmonistic alterations
- Dogmatic alterations

QUALIFYING VARIANTS

Variants can be either inconsequential (most of the variants are of this sort) or consequential in nature. Here is an example of an inconsequential variant:
- **The Masoretic text and one Septuagint (LXX) manuscript read** (author's translation):
    - 2 Samuel 24:18, "and he said to him."
- **One Qumran manuscript reads** (author's translation):
    - 2 Samuel 24:18, "and he said."
Here is an example of a consequential variant:
- **The Masoretic text reads** (author's translation):
    - 1 Samuel 25:22, "May God do thus and so to the enemies of David if by morning I leave a single male alive."
- **The Septuagint (LXX) reads** (author's translation):
    - 1 Samuel 25:22, "May God do thus and so to David if by morning I leave a single male alive."

QUANTIFYING AND UNDERSTANDING VARIANTS

Some of the early church fathers recognized differences in manuscript readings and even commented on them. As early as the third century AD, Origen wrote about preferring certain readings to others among the handwritten manuscripts he had available.[89]

---

[89] E.g., In Origen's Commentary on the Gospel According to Matthew, ser. 121 on Matthew 27:16-17 (Origen favored "Barabbas" over "Jesus Barabbas") and Commentary on the Gospel According to John VI.40 (24) on John 1:28. (Origen favored "Bethabara" over "Bethany," as the place where John the Baptist was located).

In 1707, John Mill, an English theologian at Oxford published a New Testament in Greek based on the Robertus Stephanus (1550) Greek text.[90] What was unique about this work, which was thirty years in the making, was the critical apparatus[91] with 30,000 New Testament variants catalogued. Mill had perused one hundred extant New Testament manuscripts he had available in order to develop his catalogue. This was the first attempt we have record of for a scholarly approach to quantifying variants among the biblical manuscripts.

In 1897, Eberhard Nestle produced a critical apparatus with 150,000 to 200,000 New Testament variants.[92]

Three contemporary theologians have estimated the number of variants in the New Testament alone to be between 200,000 and 500,000 total.[93]

There are a number of variants in Old Testament manuscripts. These have not been catalogued as extensively as the New Testament due to the complexity of the evidence. Some have estimated the number of variants as high as 100,000, but these numbers are problematic. Most of the so-called "variants" are actually more orthographic, i.e., related to punctuation, spelling, work breaks, etc., than substantial. Drew Longacre, postdoctoral researcher at the University of Helsinki, states, "Most of the [Old Testament] text was accurately copied down from generation to generation. Unfortunately, because of the immensity and complexity of the evidence, we will never be able to quantify the variants in the OT text."[94] Gene Ulrich, the general editor for the cave 4 Qumran manuscripts, states, "The base text of most books remained

---

[90] Adam Fox, John Mill and Richard Bentley: A Study of the Textual Criticism of the New Testament 1675–1729, (Oxford: Basil Blackwell, 1954), pp. 105–115; John Mill, Novum Testamentum Graecum, cum lectionibus variantibus MSS (Oxford, 1707).

[91] A critical apparatus is a list of key variants for the text, explaining the different manuscript readings, which ones agree, which ones differ, and how they differ. Contemporary Greek New Testaments have these critical apparatus which are not exhaustive, but explain the major discrepancies that appear in the 5,000+ manuscripts we have available today.

[92] Eberhard Nestle, Einführung in das Griechische Neue Testament, (University of California Libraries, 1909), p. 23.

[93] Bart D. Ehrman: Misquoting Jesus: The Story Behind Who Changed the Bible and Why, (New York: HarperCollins, 2005), p. 90; Eldon J. Epp, Why Does New Testament Textual Criticism Matter?, Expository Times 125 no. 9 (2014), p. 419; Peter J. Gurry, The Number of Variants in the Greek New Testament: A Proposed Estimate, New Testament Studies 62.1 (2016), p. 113.

[94] http://oldtestamenttextualcriticism.blogspot.com/2012/04/quantification-of-variants-in-ottc.html

relatively stable . . . Clearly the books were copied with a care and fidelity that fills us with awe and admiration."[95]

It is very important to understand that these "variants" are not "errors," but typically slightly different wording, the vast majority of which are inconsequential. The section below describes the impact of the variants on our English translations and how they affect the renderings.

MANUSCRIPT QUALITY DIFFERENCES

Translators of the English Bible, whatever the age, base their work on assumptions they make regarding original-language handwritten manuscript groups that have been discovered throughout the ages. For the most part, the translations developed prior to the late nineteenth century were based on relatively late Greek manuscripts from the twelfth century and later. This late manuscript group for the New Testament is called the Textus Receptus, and originated with Desiderius Erasmus, a Dutch scholar who first collected and produced an authoritative Greek manuscript of the New Testament.

In the nineteenth century, due to the exhaustive efforts of scholars, four early manuscripts, all from the fourth and fifth century were rediscovered, leading to a new comparison for the New Testament with what had been the original Greek set, as described above. Some important differences were noted. These manuscript differences are most notably reflected in the differences we see today in the Authorized Version (commonly called the "King James") English translation (based on the Textus Receptus, called the "Majority Text" because it represents the majority of ancient copies that have been found) and its subsequent editions, i.e., New King James Version and virtually all other English translations we have today (based on a range of manuscripts, including the four early manuscripts, called the "Critical Text"). See Table 6.1 for a listing of English Bible translations and their textual bases.

The differences in manuscript types between the Majority Text (MT) and the Critical Text (CT) can be seen clearly from the differences, and sometimes "missing" verses, among New Testament English translations. These differences are apparent between the King James Version, for which the translators used the Majority Text, and the New International Version, for which the translators used the Critical Text. The differences we see between the two translations are due to variants in the underlying

---

[95]Gene Ulrich, The Dead Sea Scrolls and the Origins of the Bible, (Grand Rapids: William B. Eerdmans Publishing Company, 1999), P. 109, 114

Greek manuscripts used by the translators. Below are the key verses where these variants exist:

- **Matthew 5:44**
  - MT: But I say to you, love your enemies, bless those who curse you, do good to those who hate you, and pray for those who spitefully use you and persecute you.
  - CT: But I say to you, love your enemies, and pray for those who persecute you.
- **Matthew 6:13**
  - MT: And do not lead us into temptation, But deliver us from the evil one. For Yours is the kingdom and the power and the glory forever. Amen.
  - CT: And do not lead us into temptation, But deliver us from the evil one.
- **Matthew 17:21**
  - KJV (MT): Howbeit this kind goeth not out but by prayer and fasting.
    NIV 1978 footnote (CT): But this kind does not go out except by prayer and fasting.
    NIV 2011 footnote (CT): Some manuscripts include here words similar to Mark 9:29.
  - Reason: It is possible that this verse is a duplicate of Mark 9:29.
- **Matthew 18:11**
  - KJV (MT): For the Son of man is come to save that which was lost.
    NIV 1978 footnote (CT): The Son of Man came to save what was lost.
    NIV 2011 footnote (CT): Some manuscripts include here the words of Luke 19:10.
  - Reason: According to Bruce Metzger, this verse was "manifestly borrowed by copyists from Luke 19:10.
- **Matthew 20:16**
  - MT: So the last will be first, and the first last. For many are called, but few chosen.
  - CT: So the last will be first, and the first last.

- o Matthew 20:22,23
  - MT: But Jesus answered and said, "You do not know what you ask. Are you able to drink the cup that I am about to drink, and be baptized with the baptism that I am baptized with?" They said to Him, "We are able." So He said to them, "You will indeed drink My cup, and be baptized with the baptism that I am baptized with; but to sit on My right hand and on My left is not Mine to give, but it is for those for whom it is prepared by My Father.
  - CT: But Jesus answered and said, "You do not know what you ask. Are you able to drink the cup that I am about to drink?" They said to Him, "We are able." So He said to them, "You will indeed drink My cup; but to sit on My right hand and on My left is not Mine to give, but it is for those for whom it is prepared by My Father.
- o Matthew 23:14
  - KJV (MT): Woe unto you, scribes and Pharisees, hypocrites! for ye devour widows' houses, and for a pretense make long prayer: therefore ye shall receive the greater damnation.
    NIV 1978 footnote (CT): Woe to you, teachers of the law and Pharisees, you hypocrites! You devour widows' houses and for a show make lengthy prayers. Therefore you will be punished more severely.
    NIV 2011 footnote (CT): Some manuscripts include here words similar to Mark 12:40 and Luke 20:47.
- o Matthew 24:36
  - MT: But of that day and hour no one knows, not even the angels of heaven, but My Father only.
  - CT: But of that day and hour no one knows, not even the angels of heaven, nor the Son, but My Father only.
- o Matthew 27:16
  - MT: At that time they had a notorious prisoner, called Barabbas.
  - CT: At that time they had a notorious prisoner, called [Jesus] Barabbas.
- o Mark 2:16
  - MT: "Why is He eating and drinking with tax collectors and sinners?" (see Lk 5:30)

- CT: "Why is He eating with tax collectors and sinners?"
- **Mark 6:11**
    - MT: And whoever will not receive you nor hear you, when you depart from there, shake off the dust under your feet as a testimony against them. Assuredly, I say to you, it will be more tolerable for Sodom and Gomorrah in the day of judgment than for that city!
    - CT: And whoever will not receive you nor hear you, when you depart from there, shake off the dust under your feet as a testimony against them.
- **Mark 7:8**
    - MT: For laying aside the commandment of God, you hold the tradition of men—the washing of pitchers and cups, and many other such things you do.
    - CT: For laying aside the commandment of God, you hold the tradition of men.
- **Mark 7:16**
    - KJV (MT): If any man have ears to hear, let him hear. NIV 1978 footnote (CT): If anyone has ears to hear, let him hear. NIV 2011 footnote (CT): Some manuscripts include here the words of 4:23.
- **Mark 9:44/Mark 9:46**
    - KJV (MT): Where their worm dieth not, and the fire is not quenched. NIV 1978 footnote (CT): where "their worm does not die, and the fire is not quenched." NIV 2011 footnote (CT): Some manuscripts include here the words of verse 48.
    - Reason: These two verses are identical to Mark 9:48.
    - Update: The NIV©2011 has changed their singular worm to plural: NIV 2011: 48 where "'the worms that eat them do not die, and the fire is not quenched.' Mark 9:48 Isaiah 66:24
- **Mark 9:49**
    - MT: For everyone will be seasoned with fire, and every sacrifice will be seasoned with salt.

- - CT: For everyone will be seasoned with fire.
  - o **Mark 10:24**
    - MT: And the disciples were astonished at His words. But Jesus answered again and said to them, "Children, how hard it is for those who trust in riches to enter the kingdom of God!
    - CT: And the disciples were astonished at His words. But Jesus answered again and said to them, "Children, how hard it is to enter the kingdom of God!
  - o **Mark 11:26**
    - KJV (MT): But if ye do not forgive, neither will your Father which is in heaven forgive your trespasses. NIV 1978 footnote (CT): But if you do not forgive, neither will your Father who is in heaven forgive your sins. NIV 2011 footnote (CT): Some manuscripts include here words similar to Matt. 6:15.
  - o **Mark 14:9**
    - MT: And they began to be sorrowful, and to say to Him one by one, "Is it I?" And another said, "Is it I?"
    - CT: And they began to be sorrowful, and to say to Him one by one, "Is it I?"
  - o **Mark 15:28**
    - KJV (MT): And the scripture was fulfilled, which saith, "And he was numbered with the transgressors." NIV 1978 footnote (CT): and the scripture was fulfilled which says, "He was counted with the lawless ones." NIV 2011 footnote (CT): Some manuscripts include here words similar to Luke 22:37.
  - o **Mark 16:9–20 (only in MT; omitted in the CT)**
    - 9 Now when Jesus was risen early the first day of the week, he appeared first to Mary Magdalene, out of whom he had cast seven devils.
    - 10 And she went and told them that had been with him, as they mourned and wept.
    - 11 And they, when they had heard that he was alive, and had been seen of her, believed not.
    - 12 After that he appeared in another form unto two of them, as they walked, and went into the country.

- - 13 And they went and told it unto the residue: neither believed they them.
  - 14 Afterward he appeared unto the eleven as they sat at meat, and upbraided them with their unbelief and hardness of heart, because they believed not them which had seen him after he was risen.
  - 15 And he said unto them, Go ye into all the world, and preach the gospel to every creature.
  - 16 He that believeth and is baptized shall be saved; but he that believeth not shall be damned.
  - 17 And these signs shall follow them that believe; In my name shall they cast out devils; they shall speak with new tongues;
  - 18 They shall take up serpents; and if they drink any deadly thing, it shall not hurt them; they shall lay hands on the sick, and they shall recover.
  - 19 So then after the Lord had spoken unto them, he was received up into heaven, and sat on the right hand of God.
  - 20 And they went forth, and preached every where, the Lord working with them, and confirming the word with signs following. Amen.
- o **Luke 1:28**
  - MT: And having come in, the angel said to her, "Rejoice, highly favored one, the Lord is with you; blessed are you among women!"
  - CT: And having come in, the angel said to her, "Rejoice, highly favored one, the Lord is with you!"
- o **Luke 2:14**
  - MT: "Glory to God in the highest, and on earth peace, goodwill toward men!"
  - CT: "Glory to God in the highest, and on earth peace to men on whom his favor rests."
- o **Luke 9:55-56**
  - MT: But He turned and rebuked them, and said, "You do not know what manner of spirit you are of. For the Son of Man did not come to destroy men's lives but to save them." And they went to another village.
  - CT: But He turned and rebuked them. And they went to another village.

- Luke 11:2-4
  - MT: So He said to them, "When you pray, say: Our Father in heaven, Hallowed be Your name. Your kingdom come. Your will be done On earth as it is in heaven. Give us day by day our daily bread. And forgive us our sins, For we also forgive everyone who is indebted to us. And do not lead us into temptation, But deliver us from the evil one."
  - CT: So He said to them, "When you pray, say: Father, Hallowed be Your name. Your kingdom come. Give us day by day our daily bread. And forgive us our sins, For we also forgive everyone who is indebted to us. And do not lead us into temptation."

- Luke 11:11
  - MT: If a son asks for bread from any father among you, will he give him a stone? Or if he asks for a fish, will he give him a serpent instead of a fish?
  - CT: If a son asks from any father among you for a fish, will he give him a serpent instead of a fish?

- Luke 17:36
  - KJV (MT): Two men shall be in the field; the one shall be taken, and the other left.
    NIV 1978 footnote (CT): Two men will be in the field; one will be taken and the other left.
    NIV 2011 footnote (CT): Some manuscripts include here words similar to Matt. 24:40.
  - Reason: It is possible that this verse is a duplicate of Matthew 24:40. Verse is included by very few Greek manuscripts of the Western text-type and by Old-Latin and Vulgate manuscripts.

- Luke 22:43-44
  - MT: Then an angel appeared to Him from heaven, strengthening Him. And being in agony, He prayed more earnestly. Then His sweat became like great drops of blood falling down to the ground.
  - CT: Verses marked as a later addition

- Luke 23:17
  - KJV (MT): For of necessity he must release one unto them at the feast.
    NIV 1978 footnote (CT): Now he was obliged to release one

man to them at the Feast.

NIV 2011 footnote (CT) Some manuscripts include here words similar to Matt. 27:15 and Mark 15:6.

- ○ **Luke 23:34**
  - ▪ MT: Then Jesus said, "Father, forgive them, for they do not know what they do." And they divided His garments and cast lots.
  - ▪ CT: And they divided His garments and cast lots. (*The first sentence is marked as a later addition*)
- ○ **John 1:18**
  - ▪ MT: No one has seen God at any time. The only begotten Son, who is in the bosom of the Father, He has declared Him.
  - ▪ CT: No one has seen God at any time. The only begotten God, who is in the bosom of the Father, He has declared Him.
- ○ **John 5:3–4**
  - ▪ KJV (MT): 3 In these lay a great multitude of impotent folk, of blind, halt, withered, waiting for the moving of the water. 4 For an angel went down at a certain season into the pool, and troubled the water: whosoever then first after the troubling of the water stepped in was made whole of whatsoever disease he had.
  - ▪ NIV 1978 footnote (CT): From time to time an angel of the Lord would come down and stir up the waters. The first one into the pool after each such disturbance would be cured of whatever disease he had.
  - ▪ (Note above that not only is verse 4 omitted in CT, but the tail end of verse 3 as well).
- ○ **John 6:69**
  - ▪ MT: Also we have come to believe and know that You are the Christ, the Son of the living God.
  - ▪ CT: Also we have come to believe and know that You are the Holy One of God.
- ○ **John 7:53-8:11**
  - ▪ MT: 7:53 Then they all went home
  - ▪ 8:1 but Jesus went to the Mount of Olives.
  - ▪ 2 At dawn he appeared again in the temple courts, where all the people gathered around him, and he sat down to teach them.

- 3 The teachers of the law and the Pharisees brought in a woman caught in adultery. They made her stand before the group
- 4 and said to Jesus, "Teacher, this woman was caught in the act of adultery.
- 5 In the Law Moses commanded us to stone such women. Now what do you say?"
- 6 They were using this question as a trap, in order to have a basis for accusing him. But Jesus bent down and started to write on the ground with his finger.
- 7 When they kept on questioning him, he straightened up and said to them, "Let any one of you who is without sin be the first to throw a stone at her."
- 8 Again he stooped down and wrote on the ground.
- 9 At this, those who heard began to go away one at a time, the older ones first, until only Jesus was left, with the woman still standing there.
- 10 Jesus straightened up and asked her, "Woman, where are they? Has no one condemned you?"
- 11 "No one, sir," she said. "Then neither do I condemn you," Jesus declared. "Go now and leave your life of sin."
- NIV 1978 footnote (CT): *The earliest manuscripts and many other ancient witnesses do not have John 7:53—8:11. A few manuscripts include these verses, wholly or in part, after John 7:36, John 21:25, Luke 21:38 or Luke 24:53.*
- Note: Although this verse has been proven not to have been placed after John 7:52 in the earliest manuscripts, some biblical scholars believe that it was an original oral source from the earliest followers of Jesus that was later included by scribes.

- **John 8:59**
    - MT: Then they took up stones to throw at Him; but Jesus hid Himself and went out of the temple, going through the midst of them, and so passed by.
    - CT: Then they took up stones to throw at Him; but Jesus hid Himself and went out of the temple.

- **Acts 2:30**
    - MT: Therefore, being a prophet, and knowing that God had sworn with an oath to him that of the fruit of his body, according to the flesh, He would raise up the Christ to sit on his throne

- CT: Therefore, being a prophet, and knowing that God had sworn with an oath to him that of the fruit of his body, He would seat one on his throne

- Acts 8:37

  - KJV (MT): And Philip said, If thou believest with all thine heart, thou mayest. And he answered and said, I believe that Jesus Christ is the Son of God.
  NIV 1978 footnote (CT): "If you believe with all your heart, you may." The eunuch answered, "I believe that Jesus Christ is the Son of God."

  - Reason: The earliest Greek manuscript (E^a/E_2) of the New Testament to include this verse dates from the late sixth or early seventh century and it is only found in Western witnesses to the text with many minor variations. The majority of Greek manuscripts copied after 600 AD and the majority of translations made after 600 AD do not include the verse. The tradition of the confession was current in the time of Irenaeus, as it is cited by him (c. 180) and Cyprian (c. 250)

- Acts 13:42

  - MT: So when the Jews went out of the synagogue, the Gentiles begged that these words might be preached to them the next Sabbath.

  - CT: And when they went out, they begged that these words might be preached to them the next Sabbath.

- Acts 15:24

  - MT: Since we have heard that some who went out from us have troubled you with words, unsettling your souls, saying, "You must be circumcised and keep the law" — to whom we gave no such commandment

  - CT: Since we have heard that some who went out from us have troubled you with words, unsettling your souls, to whom we gave no such commandment

- Acts 15:34

  - KJV (MT): Notwithstanding it pleased Silas to abide there still.
  NIV 1978 footnote (CT): but Silas decided to remain there

  - Reason: Majority of manuscripts do not contain this verse (only Codex Bezae, some Old-Latin and Vulgate manuscripts).

- o **Acts 18:21**
  - MT: but took leave of them, saying, "I must by all means keep this coming feast in Jerusalem; but I will return again to you, God willing." And he sailed from Ephesus.
  - CT: but took leave of them, saying, "I will return again to you, God willing." And he sailed from Ephesus.
- o **Acts 23:9**
  - MT: Then there arose a loud outcry. And the scribes of the Pharisees' party arose and protested, saying, "We find no evil in this man; but if a spirit or an angel has spoken to him, let us not fight against God."
  - CT: Then there arose a loud outcry. And the scribes of the Pharisees' party arose and protested, saying, "We find no evil in this man; what if a spirit or an angel has spoken to him?"
- o **Acts 24:6p–7**
  - KJV (MT): 6 Who also hath gone about to profane the temple: whom we took, and would have judged according to our law. 7 But the chief captain Lysias came *upon us*, and with great violence took *him* away out of our hands, 8 Commanding his accusers to come unto thee: by examining of whom thyself mayest take knowledge of all these things, whereof we accuse him.
    NIV footnote (CT): him *and wanted to judge him according to our law. 7 But the commander, Lysias, came and with the use of much force snatched him from our hands 8 and ordered his accusers to come before you.*
  - (Note above that not only is verse 7 omitted in CT, but also the end of verse 6 and beginning of verse 8.)
- o **Acts 28:29**
  - KJV (MT): And when he had said these words, the Jews departed, and had great reasoning among themselves.
    NIV 1978 footnote (CT): After he said this, the Jews left, arguing vigorously among themselves.
- o **Romans 8:1**
  - MT: There is therefore now no condemnation to those who are in Christ Jesus, who do not walk according to the flesh, but according to the Spirit.

- CT: There is therefore now no condemnation to those who are in Christ Jesus.

o **Romans 10:15**

- MT: And how shall they preach unless they are sent? As it is written: "How beautiful are the feet of those who preach the gospel of peace, Who bring glad tidings of good things!"
- CT: And how shall they preach unless they are sent? As it is written: "How beautiful are the feet of those who bring glad tidings of good things!"

o **Romans 11:16**

- MT: And if by grace, then it is no longer of works; otherwise grace is no longer grace. But if it is of works, it is no longer grace; otherwise work is no longer work.
- CT: And if by grace, then it is no longer of works; otherwise grace is no longer grace.

o **Romans 14:6**

- MT: He who observes the day, observes it to the Lord; and he who does not observe the day, to the Lord he does not observe it. He who eats, eats to the Lord, for he gives God thanks; and he who does not eat, to the Lord he does not eat, and gives God thanks.
- CT: He who observes the day, observes it to the Lord. He who eats, eats to the Lord, for he gives God thanks; and he who does not eat, to the Lord he does not eat, and gives God thanks.

o **Romans 16:24**

- KJV (MT): The grace of our Lord Jesus Christ be with you all. Amen.
  NIV 1978 footnote (CT): May the grace of our Lord Jesus Christ be with all of you. Amen

o **1 Corinthians 6:20**

- MT: For you were bought at a price; therefore glorify God in your body and in your spirit, which are God's.
- CT: For you were bought at a price; therefore glorify God in your body

- o **1 Corinthians 9:20**
  - MT: and to the Jews I became as a Jew, that I might win Jews; to those who are under the law, as under the law, that I might win those who are under the law
  - CT: and to the Jews I became as a Jew, that I might win Jews; to those who are under the law, as under the law, though not being myself under the law that I might win those who are under the law

- o **1 Corinthians 14:38**
  - MT: But if anyone is ignorant, let him be ignorant.
  - CT: But if anyone does not recognize this, he is not recognized.

- o **Galatians 3:1**
  - MT: O foolish Galatians! Who has bewitched you that you should not obey the truth, before whose eyes Jesus Christ was clearly portrayed among you as crucified?
  - CT: O foolish Galatians! Who has bewitched you before whose eyes Jesus Christ was clearly portrayed among you as crucified?

- o **Ephesians 5:30**
  - MT: For we are members of His body, of His flesh and of His bones.
  - CT: For we are members of His body.

- o **Philippians 3:16**
  - MT: Nevertheless, to the degree that we have already attained, let us walk by the same rule, let us be of the same mind.
  - CT: Nevertheless, to the degree that we have already attained, let us walk by the same.

- o **1 Timothy 3:16**
  - MT: And without controversy great is the mystery of godliness: God was manifested in the flesh, justified in the Spirit, seen by angels, preached among the Gentiles, believed on in the world, received up in glory.
  - CT: By common confession, great is the mystery of godliness: He who was revealed in the flesh, was vindicated in the Spirit, seen by angels, proclaimed among the nations, believed on in the world, taken up in glory.

- ○ **1 Timothy 6:5**
  - ▪ MT: useless wranglings of men of corrupt minds and destitute of the truth, who suppose that godliness is a means of gain. From such withdraw yourself.
  - ▪ CT: useless wranglings of men of corrupt minds and destitute of the truth, who suppose that godliness is a means of gain
- ○ **Hebrews 10:34**
  - ▪ MT: for you had compassion on me in my chains, and joyfully accepted the plundering of your goods, knowing that you have a better and an enduring possession for yourselves in heaven.
  - ▪ CT: for you had compassion on the prisoners, and joyfully accepted the plundering of your goods, knowing that you have a better and an enduring possession for yourselves in heaven.
- ○ **1 Peter 2:2**
  - ▪ MT: as newborn babes, desire the pure milk of the word, that you may grow thereby
  - ▪ CT: as newborn babes, desire the pure milk of the word, that you may grow thereby up to salvation
- ○ **1 Peter 4:14**
  - ▪ MT: If you are reproached for the name of Christ, blessed are you, for the Spirit of glory and of God rests upon you. On their part He is blasphemed, but on your part He is glorified.
  - ▪ CT: If you are reproached for the name of Christ, blessed are you, for the Spirit of glory and of God rests upon you.
- ○ **2 Peter 1:21**
  - ▪ MT: for prophecy never came by the will of man, but holy men of God spoke as they were moved by the Holy Spirit.
  - ▪ CT: for prophecy never came by the will of man, but men spoke from God as they were moved by the Holy Spirit.
- ○ **1 John 3:1**
  - ▪ MT: Behold what manner of love the Father has bestowed on us, that we should be called children of God! Therefore the world does not know us, because it did not know Him.
  - ▪ CT: Behold what manner of love the Father has bestowed on us, that we should be called children of God! And we are. Therefore the world does not know us, because it did not know Him.

- **1 John 4:3**
  - MT: and every spirit that does not confess that Jesus Christ has come in the flesh is not of God. And this is the spirit of the Antichrist, which you have heard was coming, and is now already in the world.
  - CT: and every spirit that does not confess Jesus is not of God. And this is the spirit of the Antichrist, which you have heard was coming, and is now already in the world.
- **1 John 5:13**
  - MT: These things I have written to you who believe in the name of the Son of God, that you may know that you have eternal life, and that you may continue to believe in the name of the Son of God.
  - CT: These things I have written to you who believe in the name of the Son of God, that you may know that you have eternal life.
- **Jude 22-23**
  - MT: And on some have compassion, making a distinction; but others save with fear, pulling them out of the fire, hating even the garment defiled by the flesh.
  - CT: And on some have compassion, who are doubting; but others save, pulling them out of the fire, and on some have mercy with fear hating even the garment defiled by the flesh.
- **Jude 25**
  - MT: To God our Savior, Who alone is wise, Be glory and majesty, Dominion and power, Both now and forever. Amen.
  - CT: To the only God our Savior, through Jesus Christ our Lord, Be glory and majesty, Dominion and power, Before all time, now and forever. Amen.
- **Rev 22:14**
  - MT: Blessed are those who do His commandments, that they may have the right to the tree of life, and may enter through the gates into the city.
  - CT: Blessed are those who wash their robes, that they may have the right to the tree of life, and may enter through the gates into the city.

HOW DOES THE BIBLE STACK UP OVER TIME? A COMPARISON TO OTHER WORKS

The Bible is unique among the literary works of the ages. The following table makes a comparison between the New Testament and other works of antiquity with regard to transmission over time and accuracy of the copies. For example, the earliest extant copy of the works of Sophocles, which are dated to the 5th century BC, is from the 11th century AD. That means 1,400 years exist between the estimated time of writing and the earliest copy we have today. We have 193 copies, but how can we know how with any certainty about the accuracy of these copies?

Homer's *Iliad* is the next most prolific work besides the New Testament to survive today. Note that the approximate time between the writing and the earliest known copy is 500 years. That would be comparable to someone today producing a copy of a work of Martin Luther from the 16th century Reformation era. We simply do not know what the copy is based upon, or any idea of the accuracy of the copy given the lack of intermediate editions.

It turns out the New Testament is the most reliable of the ancient literary works to survive antiquity. Table 5.1 below is a summary of the major works of antiquity compared to the New Testament. It shows that the New Testament copies we have today far outnumber the next most prolific work, and the copies we have are much closer to the time of the original. Appendix G shows a more comprehensive table with more ancient works.

Table 5.1. The New Testament compared with other significant works of antiquity.

Author	Work	Date	Earliest Extant Copy	Approx Time between original & copy	Copies Available Today	Accuracy
Various	New Testament	1st Cent. A.D. (50-100 A.D.	2nd Cent. A.D. (c. 130 A.D. f.)	less than 100 years	5800+	99.50%
Homer	Iliad	900 B.C.	400 B.C.	500 years	643	95%
Sophocles	Various plays	496-406 B.C.	1000 A.D.	1400 years	193	- - - -
Aristotle	Corpus Aristotelicum	384-322 B.C.	1100 A.D.	1400 years	49	- - - -
Euripides	Various plays	480-406 B.C.	1100 A.D.	1300 years	9	- - - -
Demosthenes	Various orations	4th Cent. B.C.	1100 A.D.	800 years	8	- - - -
Plato	Dialogues	427-347 B.C.	900 A.D.	1200 years	7	- - - -

THE NEW TESTAMENT AND THE WRITINGS OF SHAKESPEARE

The New Testament can be compared to the works of William Shakespeare (1564-1616). We have had the plays of Shakespeare around for the last 400 years. They were produced in the age of printing, and so had the advantage (or perhaps disadvantage) of proliferation and ease of access. Yet, even with these characteristics, in each of his 37 plays there are about 100 readings still in dispute among scholars which affect the meaning of the lines. In Table 5.2 below, we can see the wide divergence of quality and transmittance of both the New Testament books and the works of Shakespeare. Even with the "advantage" of printing with moveable type, the quality of Shakespeare's works was not maintained throughout the past few hundred years.

Table 5.2. The New Testament compared to the works of William Shakespeare

New Testament	William Shakespeare
In existence about 1,900 years	In existence less than 400 years
First approximately 15 centuries, copied by hand	Copied by printing press
Only about 20 significant textual variations, and none affect key Christian doctrine	In each of his 37 plays, there are about 100 readings still in dispute; a large number substantially affect meaning

CHAPTER 6
ENGLISH BIBLE
TRANSLATIONS

WHAT ABOUT TRANSLATIONS?

Three primary characteristics underlie a majority of the differences we see in the language of our English translations. The first reflects cultural changes that take place over time and place. The second characteristic has to do with the purpose behind the translation, whether it follows the original language closely or is more "dynamic" for the purpose of reaching a certain type of reader or for more devotional reading. The third is due to variants in the underlying Greek manuscripts used by the translators, as we learned in Chapter 5.

CULTURAL CHANGES

Every language changes over time generally, and specifically by age and cultural group and geography to various degrees. Colloquial English, for instance, changes continually within generations and cultural groups, and from place to place. General cultural changes in language can be shown in a popular English translation, the New International Version (NIV). There have been changes in the translation over time to reflect some changes in culture. The original NIV was produced in 1978. Since that time there have been two revisions, one in 1984 and one in 2011.

Here are examples of the differences in the NIV, notably the 2011 revision with "inclusive" language versus the New King James Version (NKJV):

Psalm 8:4:
- NKJV: "What is man that You are mindful of him, And the son of man that You visit him?"
- NIV 1978, 1984: "what is man that you are mindful of him, the son of man that you care for him?"
- NIV 2011: "what is mankind that you are mindful of them, human beings that you care for them?"

TRANSLATION PURPOSE

Since the Bible is the best-selling book of all time, it makes sense for marketing purposes to change the translation to fit not only cultural mores like inclusiveness, but also the language changes that reach particular English-speaking people groups and for the purposes of assisting with study, devotions, particular points of view, etc. Hence we have Bibles such as the New International Reader's Version (NIrV), which simplifies syntax and was designed for a third grade reading level, the English Standard Version (ESV), which was designed for pastors and teachers with a literal rendering, and New English Translation (NET), which enhances study. The Message (MSG) was developed to bring vitality and directness to Bible reading. The Inclusive Bible seeks to be the first "egalitarian" translation by using "new and non-sexist ways to express ancient truths." No doubt there will be many more new translations to come.

TYPES OF TRANSLATIONS

As regards translation itself, there is a range of types that describe how close the text follows the original language, or the closest thing to the original we have such as ancient Hebrew or Greek manuscripts, or how close the text follows the original thoughts or ideas. One end of the spectrum is called "formal equivalence" which means the translators attempt to remain as close to the original text or idea as possible, even when the text appears stilted or unclear. These translations are designed to be word-for-word translations. Examples would include the New American Standard and the King James Version. On the other end of the spectrum is what is called "dynamic equivalence" which means the text provides the essence of the original text, usually in a paraphrase style. Translators seek to maintain a sense-for-sense style. Examples of dynamic equivalence translation type include paraphrases such as The Message Bible, The Living Bible, or the Good News Bible. Of course, there are a number of translations that range between the dynamic and formal types.

Some would say that if we want to study the Bible closest to its original form, we should have a formal equivalence bible handy. Certainly for study and doctrinal discussions, we must use the formal equivalence translations. Similarly, if we would like a more devotional approach that flows with modern English culture, we might choose a dynamic equivalent translation. No one translation style will fit all needs and all types of people. The best approach is to understand the type of translations and choose those that fit our particular needs.

The table below includes a range of popular English translations today and where they fit in the translation style continuum.

Table 6.1. The Spectrum of English Bible Translations and Types.

Translation Name	Date	Translation Type	Textual Basis
King James Version (KJV)*	1611	Formal Equivalence	NT: TR, VG OT: MT DC/Apoc: LXX, VG
New King James Version (NKJV)*	1982	Formal Equivalence	NT: TR OT: MT, LXX
Revised Standard Version (RSV)	1952	Formal Equivalence	NT: NA OT: BHS, DSS, LXX DC/Apoc: LXX, VG
New Revised Standard Version (RSV)	1989	Formal Equivalence	NT: NA27 OT: BHS, DSS, LXX DC/Apoc: LXX, VG
American Standard Version (ASV)	1901	Formal Equivalence	NT: WH OT: MT, LXX
New American Standard Version (NASV)	1995	Formal Equivalence	NT: NA OT: BHS, LXX
English Standard Version (ESV)	2001	Formal Equivalence	NT: NA27 OT: BHS4, LXX DC/Apoc: LXX, VG
New International Version (NIV)	1978	Formal-Dynamic "Optimal" equivalence	NT: NA OT: BHS, MT, DSS, VG, SP, Aq, SyTh, SyP, AT
New English Translation (NET)	2005	Formal-Dynamic "Optimal" equivalence	NT: NA27 OT: BHS4, LXX (60,932 translator notes!)
Holman Christian Standard Bible (HCSB)	2004	Formal-Dynamic "Optimal" equivalence	NT:NA27, UBS4 OT: BHS4, LXX
New Living Translation (NLT)	1996	Formal-Dynamic "Optimal" equivalence	NT: UBS4, NA27 OT: BHS, LXX
Amplified Bible (AMP)	1965	Formal-Dynamic "Optimal" equivalence	NT: WH OT: MT, LXX
New English Bible (NEB)	1970	Dynamic-Paraphrase	NT: Eclectic. OT: MT/BHS, DSS, SP, LXX, AT, SyP
Good News Bible (GNB)	1976	Dynamic-Paraphrase	NT: NA27 OT: MT
The Living Bible (TLB)	1971	Dynamic-Paraphrase	Paraphrase of ASV with KJV
The Message (MSG)	2002	Dynamic-Paraphrase	NT: Eclectic OT: Eclectic
New Jerusalem Bible (NJB)	1985	Dynamic-Paraphrase	NT: NA25 OT: BHS,, LXX DC/Apoc: LXX, VG

*Note that only two English translations, the KJV and NKJV, rely on the Textus Receptus (TR, or "Majority Text," meaning translators used late manuscripts only) for the New Testament. The NKJV translators typically provide marginal notes that explain where the Majority Text differs from the Critical Text.

Explanations of the abbreviations:

NT: New Testament

OT: Old Testament

NA27: Nestle-Aland 27th edition Greek New Testament (based on the Critical Text, CT)

UBS4: United Bible Society 4th edition Greek New Testament (based on the Critical Text, CT)

WH: Westcott and Hort 1881

BHS4: Biblia Hebraica Stuttgartensia Hebrew Old Testament 4th edition

VG: Vulgate

LXX: Septuagint

DC/Apoc: Deuterocanon/Apocrypha

MT: Masoretic Text (Old Testament)

TR: Textus Receptus (New Testament, based on the Majority Text. MT)

DSS: Dead Sea Scrolls

SP: Samaritan Pentateuch

Aq: Aquila

SyTh: Symmachus and Theodotion

SyP: Syriac Peshitta

AT: Aramaic Targums

APPENDIX A: THE NICENE CREED

(325 A.D.; revised at Constantinople, 381 A.D.)

I believe in one God the Father Almighty; Maker of heaven and earth, and of all things visible and invisible. And in one Lord Jesus Christ, the only-begotten Son of God, begotten of the Father before all worlds, God of God, Light of Light, very God of very God, begotten, not made, being of one substance with the Father; by whom all things were made; who, for us men and for our salvation, came down from heaven, and was incarnate by the Holy Spirit of the Virgin Mary, and was made man; and was crucified also for us under Pontius Pilate ; he suffered and was buried; and the third day he rose again, according to the Scriptures; and ascended into heaven, and sitteth on the right hand of the Father; and he shall come again, with glory, to judge both the quick and the dead; whose kingdom shall have no end. And in the Holy Spirit, the Lord and Giver of Life; who proceedeth from the Father and the Son; who with the Father and the Son together is worshipped and glorified; who spake by the Prophets. And one Holy catholic and Apostolic Church. I acknowledge one Baptism for the remission of sins; and I look for the resurrection of the dead, and the life of the world to come. Amen.

APPENDIX B: CHRISTIAN GROUPS OVER TIME AND THEIR RELATIONSHIPS

by, Michael J. Chenevey

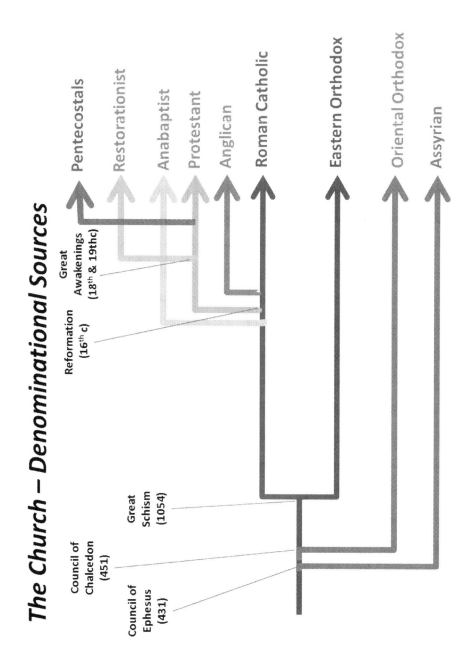

APPENDIX C: THE USE OF THE APOCRYPHA AMONG VARIOUS CHRISTIAN GROUPS

by, Michael J. Chenevey

Major Denomination	Canonical Books	Apocrypha/Deuterocanon Books	Notes
Roman Catholic (RC; follow 4th c Vulgate)	OT, 46 books NT, 27 books		
		Tobit	
		Judith	
		Additions to Esther (Vulgate Esther 10:4-16:24)	
		Wisdom	
		Sirach, also called Ben Sira or Ecclesiasticus	
		Baruch, including the Letter of Jeremiah (Additions to Jeremiah in the Septuagint)	
		Additions to Daniel:	
		Prayer of Azariah and Song of the Three Holy Children (Vulgate Daniel 3:24-90)	
		Susanna (Vulgate Daniel 13, Septuagint prologue)	
		Bel and the Dragon (Vulgate Daniel 14, Septuagint epilogue)	
		1 Maccabees	
		2 Maccabees	
Protestantism (split with RC in the 16th c)		(Apocrypha from Vulgate)	
Baptist	OT, 39 books NT, 27 books	Historically include the deuterocanon (as RC) as an appendix	
Methodist	Same	Historically include the deuterocanon (as RC) as an appendix	
Lutheran	Same	Historically include the deuterocanon (as RC) as an appendix	

Major Denomination List	Canon	Apocrypha/Deuterocanon	Notes
Reformed	Same	Historically include the deuterocanon (as RC) as an appendix	The Belgic Confession, used in Reformed churches, devotes a section (Article 6) to "The difference between the canonical and apocryphal books" and asserts that "All which the Church may read and take instruction from, so far as they agree with the canonical books; but they are far from having such power and efficacy as that we may from their testimony confirm any point of faith or of the Christian religion; much less to detract from the authority of the other sacred books."
Presbyterian	Same	None	Westminster Confession: Chapter 1, Article 3 reads: "The books commonly called Apocrypha, not being of divine inspiration, are no part of the Canon of Scripture; and therefore are of no authority in the Church of God, nor to be any otherwise approved, or made use of, than other human writings."
Congregationalism	Same	Historically include the deuterocanon (as RC) as an appendix	
Anabaptists	Same	Historically include the deuterocanon (as RC) as an appendix	
Pentecostals	Same	Historically include the deuterocanon (as RC) as an appendix	
Evangelicals	Same	Historically include the deuterocanon (as RC) as an appendix	
Christian & Missionary Alliance	Same	Historically include the deuterocanon (as RC) as an appendix	

Major Denomination List	Canon	Apocrypha/Deuterocanon	Notes
African initiated	Same	Historically include the deuterocanon (as RC) as an appendix	
Seventh day Adventist	Same	Historically include the deuterocanon (as RC) as an appendix	
Restoration Movement (Churches of Christ)	Same	Historically include the deuterocanon (as RC) as an appendix	
Eastern Orthodox (Follow 3rd c BC Septuagint)	OT, 49 books NT, 27 books	Anagignoskomena (what Orthodox call the deuterocanon)	
		To the Roman list, add 3 Maccabees and 1 Esdras (also included in the Clementine Vulgate), while Baruch is divided from the Epistle of Jeremiah, making a total of 49 Old Testament books	
		Orthodox usu. also add: Psalm 151, Prayer of Manasses, and include 4 Maccabees (Greek), 2 Esdras (Slavonic) as an appendix	
Oriental Orthodoxy	OT, 49 books NT, 27 books	Same as above	
		Amharic (Semitic language) Bible used by the Ethiopian and Eritrean Orthodox Churches also includes some books that are still held canonical by only the Ethiopian Church, including Enoch or Henok (I Enoch), Kufale (Jubilees) and 1, 2 and 3 Meqabyan (not Maccabees)	

Anglicanism	OT, 39 books NT, 27 books		
		The Apocrypha section of the original 1611 King James Bible includes, in addition to the deuterocanonical books (RC canon), the following three books, which were not included in the list of the canonical books by the Council of Trent: * 1 Esdras (Vulgate 3 Esdras) * 2 Esdras (Vulgate 4 Esdras) * Prayer of Manasses	The Church of England lists the deuterocanonical books as suitable to be read for "example of life and instruction of manners, but yet doth net apply them to establish any doctrine."

Source: *http://en.wikipedia.org/wiki/Deuterocanonical_books*

APPENDIX D: BOOKS OF THE BIBLE

Old Testament

Books	Hebrew Transliteration	Translation	Author	Source (Author)	Date written	Canon/ Traditions	Notes
Torah (Law)							
Genesis	Beresheet	In the Beginning	Moses	Jewish tradition	? - 1445 BC	RC, P, EO, OO, A	
Exodus	Shemot	Names	Moses	Jewish tradition	1445-1405 BC	RC, P, EO, OO, A	
Leviticus	Vayikra	And He Called	Moses	Jewish tradition	1405 BC	RC, P, EO, OO, A	
Numbers	Bemidvar	In the Desert	Moses	Jewish tradition	1444-1405 BC	RC, P, EO, OO, A	
Deuteronomy	Devarim	Words	Moses	Jewish tradition	1405 BC	RC, P, EO, OO, A	
Nevi'im (Prophets)							
Joshua	Yehoshua	Yah Saves	Joshua	Jewish tradition	1404-1390 BC	RC, P, EO, OO, A	
Judges	Shofetim	Judges	Samuel	Jewish tradition	1374-1129 BC	RC, P, EO, OO, A	
Samuel	Shamuel	Heard By God	Samuel	Jewish tradition	1043-1004 BC	RC, P, EO, OO, A	
Kings	Malachim	Kings	Jeremiah	Jewish tradition	971-587 BC	RC, P, EO, OO, A	
"Latter Prophets"							
Isaiah	Yesha'yah	Yah is Salvation	Isaiah	Jewish tradition	740-680 BC	RC, P, EO, OO, A	8th c – Babylonian captivity
Jeremiah	Yirmi'yah	Yah Lifts Up	Jeremiah & Baruch	Jewish tradition	627-585 BC	RC, P, EO, OO, A	6th c – Assyrian captivity
Ezekiel	Y'chizki'el	God Strengthens	Ezekiel	Jewish tradition	593-560 BC	RC, P, EO, OO, A	6th c – Assyrian captivity

Books	Hebrew Transliteration	Translation	Author	Source (Author)	Date written	Traditions*	Notes
"Minor Prophets" (12)							*Single book in the Hebrew Bible; "Book of the Twelve"*
Hosea	Hoshea	Yah Save	Hosea son of Beeri	Jewish tradition	755-715 BC	RC, P, EO, OO, A	Northern kingdom (Israel)
Joel	Yo'el	Yah is God	Joel son of Pethuel	Jewish tradition	835-796 BC	RC, P, EO, OO, A	N/A
Amos	Amos ("Ah-mose")	Burden Bearer	Amos of Tekoa	Jewish tradition	765-750 BC	RC, P, EO, OO, A	Herdsman and farmer, southern kingdom (Judah)
Obadiah	Oved'yah	Servant of Yah	Obadiah	Jewish tradition	840 BC	RC, P, EO, OO, A	Southern kingdom (Judah)
Jonah	Yonah	Dove	Jonah, son of Amittai	Jewish tradition	780-850 BC	RC, P, EO, OO, A	Northern kingdom (Israel)
Micah	Mikhah (Mikhayah)	Who is Like Yah	Micah of Moresheth	Jewish tradition	740-690 BC	RC, P, EO, OO, A	Southern kingdom (Judah)
Nahum	Nachum	Comforter	Nahum, the Elkoshite	Jewish tradition	630-612 BC	RC, P, EO, OO, A	Southern kingdom (Judah)?
Habakkuk	Chav'kuk	Embracer	Habakkuk	Jewish tradition	606-604 BC	RC, P, EO, OO, A	Southern kingdom (Judah)?
Zephaniah	Zefan'yah	Yah Hides	Zephaniah, son of Cushi	Jewish tradition	625 BC	RC, P, EO, OO, A	Southern kingdom (Judah)

Books	Hebrew Transliteration	Translation	Author	Source (Author)	Date written	Traditions*	Notes
Haggai	Chagi	My Feast	Haggai	Jewish tradition	520 BC	RC, P, EO, OO, A	Persian period (post-exilic)
Zechariah	Zachar'yah	Yah Remembers	Zechariah, son of Berekiah	Jewish tradition	515 BC	RC, P, EO, OO, A	Persian period (post-exilic)
Malachi	Malakhi	My Messenger	Malachi (or Nehemiah?)	Jewish tradition	430 BC	RC, P, EO, OO, A	Persian period (post-exilic)
Ketuvim ("Writings")							
Psalms	T'hilim	Praises	Various	N/A	Unknown	RC, P, EO, OO, A	
Job	Yob	Hostility	Unknown	Unknown	Unknown	RC, P, EO, OO, A	May be earliest work in OT
Proverbs	Mashali	My Rule/Wisdom	Various	N/A	950-700 BC	RC, P, EO, OO, A	
Ruth	Rut	Chained/Welded	Samuel	Talmud	1150 BC?	RC, P, EO, OO, A	
Song of Songs (or Song of Solomon)	Shir Hashirim	The Song of Songs	Solomon	Jewish tradition	960-970 BC	RC, P, EO, OO, A	
Ecclesiastes (or Qoheleth)	Kehilat	Community	Solomon or "Qoheleth"	Jewish tradition	930-940 BC	RC, P, EO, OO, A	
Lamentations	Akhah	How?	Jeremiah	Jewish tradition	586 BC	RC, P, EO, OO, A	

Books	Hebrew Transliteration	Translation	Author	Source (Author)	Date written	Traditions*	Notes
Esther	Bab: Estare, Heb: Hadasah	"Star", "Myrtle Tree"	Unknown (Mordecai?)	Josephus	464-415 BC	RC, P, EO, OO, A	Persian period (post-exilic)
Daniel	Dani'el	God is My Judge	Daniel	Jewish tradition	605-536 BC	RC, P, EO, OO, A	Babylon ian period (8th c)
Ezra	Ezra	Help	Ezra	Jewish tradition	538-520 BC	RC, P, EO, OO, A	Persian period (post-exilic); Ezra-Nehemi ah = 1 & 2 Esdras in Vulgate
Nehemiah	Nacham'yah	Yah Comforts	Nehemiah	Jewish tradition	445-425 BC	RC, P, EO, OO, A	Persian period (post-exilic)
Chronicles	Davari Hayamim	Word of the Ages	Ezra?	N/A	450-425 BC	RC, P, EO, OO, A	

Sources: _http://bible.org/seriespage/minor-prophets; http://carm.org/when-was-bible-written-and-who-wrote-it_

Deuterocanon (Primarily from Septuagint)

Books	Greek Transliteration	Translation	Author	Source (Author)	Date written	Traditions*	Notes
Tobit	Tobit	My good	Tobias		250 - 175 BC	RC, P, EO, OO, A	
Judith	Joudith		Unknown		175 - 110 BC	RC, P, EO, OO, A	
Additions to Esther	Esther				180 - 145 BC		

Books	Greek Transliteration	Translation	Author	Source (Author)	Date written	Traditions*	Notes
Wisdom	Sophia Salomon		(Likely an Alexandrian Jew)		150 BC – 40 AD	RC, P, EO, OO, A	
Sirach, also called Ben Sira or Ecclesiasticus	Sophia Seirax		Ben Sira		190–175 BC	RC, P, EO, OO, A	
Baruch, including the Letter of Jeremiah	Baroux, Epistole Jeremiou		Baruch (scribe of Jeremiah)		200 BC – 70 AD	RC, P, EO, OO, A	
1 Esdras	Esdras A		Ezra (Pseudonym?)		150 BC?	EO, OO, A	= 3 Esdras in Vulgate; not in RC canon
2 Esdras	Esdras B		Ezra (Pseudonym?)		70 – 135 AD	EO, OO, A	= 4 Esdras in Vulgate; not in Septuagint
Additions to Daniel:							
Prayer of Azariah and Song of the Three Holy Children	Ton Trion Paidon Ainesis	The Three Children Praise			167 – 163 BC	RC, P, EO, OO, A	Daniel 3:24-90 in Vulgate
Susanna	Susanna				100 BC?	RC, P, EO, OO, A	Daniel 13 in Vulgate
Bel and the Dragon	Bel and Drakon				150 – 100 BC	RC, P, EO, OO, A	Daniel 14 in Vulgate

Books	Greek/Amharic Transliteration	Translation	Author	Source (Author)	Date written	Traditions*	Notes
1 Maccabees	Makkabaion A		Unknown		103 – 63 BC	RC, P, EO, OO, A	
2 Maccabees	Makkabaion B		Jason of Cyrene?		100 BC?	RC, P, EO, OO, A	
3 Maccabees	Makkabaion G				100 BC – 0 AD	EO, OO	Not in RC canon
4 Maccabees	Makkabaion D		Unknown		Unknown	EO, OO	Not in RC canon
Prayer of Manasseh	Proseuxe Manasse		Manasses, King of Judah		150 – 50 BC	EO, OO, A	Not in RC canon
Psalm 151	Psalmoi 151		Unknown		Unknown	EO, OO	Not in RC canon; not in Septuagint
Enoch (or Henok)	Henok	Enoch	N/A	N/A	N/A	OO	Amharic (Semitic language); used by Ethiopian & Eritrean Orthodox Churches
Kufale (Jubilees)	Kufale	Jubilees	N/A	N/A	N/A	OO	Same as above
1 Meqabyan	Meqabyan I	N/A	N/A	N/A	N/A	OO	Same as above
2 Meqabyan	Meqabyan II	N/A	N/A	N/A	N/A	OO	Same as above
3 Meqabyan	Meqabyan III	N/A	N/A	N/A	N/A	OO	Same as above

Sources: http://www.newadvent.org/cathen/01601a.htm#I; H. Wayne House, 1981, Chronological and Background Charts of the New Testament, Grand Rapids: Zondervan

Books	Greek Transliteration	Translation	Author	Source (Author)	Date written	Traditions *	Notes
Matthew	Kata Mathaion	According to Matit'yahu (Levi)	Matthew	Internal	60's AD	All	Synoptic Gospel
Mark	Kata Markon	According to Markos	John Mark	Tradition	late 50's - early 60's AD	All	Synoptic Gospel
Luke	Kata Loukan	According to Lukan	Luke	Tradition	60 AD	All	Synoptic Gospel
John	Kata Ioannen	According to Yochanon	John the Apostle	Tradition	late 80's - early 90's AD	All	"Fourth" Gospel (late)
Acts	Praxeis Apostolon	Acts of the Apostles	Luke	Tradition	61 AD	All	
Romans	Pros Romaious	To Romans	Paul	Internal	55 AD	All	
1 Corinthians	Pros Korinthious A	To Corinthians 1	Paul	Internal	54 AD	All	
2 Corinthians	Pros Korinthious B	To Corinthians 2	Paul	Internal	55 AD	All	
Galatians	Pros Galatas	To Galatians	Paul	Internal	49 AD	All	
Ephesians	Pros Ephesious	To Ephesians	Paul	Internal	60 AD	All	
Philippians	Pros Philippesious	To Philippians	Paul	Internal	61 AD	All	
Colossians	Pros Kolossaeis	To Colossians	Paul	Internal	60 AD	All	
1 Thessalonians	Pros Thessalonikeis A	To Thessalonians 1	Paul	Internal	50-51 AD	All	
2 Thessalonians	Pros Thessalonikeis B	To Thessalonians 2	Paul	Internal	50-51 AD	All	

New Testament

Books	Greek Transliteration	Translation	Author	Source (Author)	Date written	Traditions*	Notes
1 Timothy	Pros Timotheon A	To Timothy 1	Paul	Internal	62 AD	All	
2 Timothy	Pros Timotheon B	To Timothy 2	Paul	Internal	63 AD	All	
Titus	Pros Titon	To Titus	Paul	Internal	62 AD	All	
Hebrews	Pros Hebraious	To Hebrews	Paul, Apollo, or Barnabas ?	Tradition	60's AD	All	
James	Iakobou	Jacob (Ya'akov)	James, brother of Jesus	Internal	40's or 50's AD	All	
1 Peter	Petrou A	Peter 1	Peter	Internal	63 AD	All	
2 Peter	Petrou B	Peter 2	Peter	Internal	63-64 AD	All	
1 John	Ioannou A	John 1	John the Apostle	Tradition	late 80's – early 90's AD	All	
2 John	Ioannou B	John 2	John the Apostle	Tradition	late 80's – early 90's AD	All	
3 John	Ioannou G	John 3	John the Apostle	Tradition	late 80's – early 90's AD	All	
Jude	Iouda	Y'hudah	Jude, brother of Jesus	Internal	60's or 70's AD	All	

Books	Greek Transliteration	Translation	Author	Source (Author)	Date written	Traditions*	Notes
Revelation	Apokalupsis Ioannou	Revelation of John	John the Apostle	Internal	late 80's – early 90's AD	All	
Chronological Order (Appx)							
Galatians					49 AD		
1 Thessalonians					50-51 AD		
2 Thessalonians					50-51 AD		
1 Corinthians					54 AD		
2 Corinthians					55 AD		
Romans					55 AD		
James					40's or 50's AD		
Mark					late 50's – early 60's AD		
Philemon					60 AD		
Colossians					60 AD		
Ephesians					60 AD		
Luke					60 AD		
Acts					61 AD		
Philippians					61 AD		
1 Timothy					62 AD		
Titus					62 AD		

Books	Greek Transliteration	Translation	Author	Source (Author)	Date written	Traditions*	Notes
2 Timothy					63 AD		
1 Peter					63 AD		
2 Peter					63-64 AD		
Matthew					60's AD		
Hebrews					60's AD		
Jude					60's or 70's AD		
John					late 80's - early 90's AD		
1 John					late 80's - early 90's AD		
2 John					late 80's - early 90's AD		
3 John					late 80's - early 90's AD		
Revelation					late 80's - early 90's AD		
* Traditions: RC = Roman Catholic; P = Protestant; A = Anglican (Episcopal); EO = Eastern Orthodox; OO = Oriental Orthodox							

APPENDIX E: THE NON-CANONICAL APOCRYPHAL WORKS

by, Michael J. Chenevey

Apocryphal Works (Non-Canonical)

Jewish Origin	Date (estimate)	Notes
Apocalyptic works		
The Book of Henoch (Ethiopic)	170-95 BC	Mentioned in Jude 14-15
Assumption of Moses	4 BC - 10 AD	Mentioned in Jude 9
Book of the Secrets of Henoch (Slavonic Henoch)	??	
Fourth Book of Esdras	< 218 AD	Called 2 Esdras by non-Catholics
Apocalypse of Baruch	50-117 AD	
The Apocalypse of Abraham	??	
The Apocalypse of Daniel	??	
Legendary Apocryphal works		
Book of Jubilees or Little Genesis	135 BC - 60 AD	St Jerome mentions
The Book of Jannes and Mambres		Names mentioned in 2 Tim 3:8; Origin mentions the work
Third Book of Esdras	300 BC - 100 AD	Called 1 Esdras by non-Catholics; included in Vaticanus and Alexandrinus. Mentioned by early fathers as Scripture; rejected by Jerome
Third Book of Machabees	100 BC - 100 AD	found in the Alexandrine codex; included in Greek Orthodox canon
Apocryphal psalms and prayers		
Psalms of Solomon	63 BC	18 Hebrew psalms
Prayer of Manasses (Manasseh)	??	based on II Paralipomenon, 33:11-13
Jewish philosophy		
Fourth Book of Machabees	??	Four "cardinal virtues" derived from this work

Christian Origin	Date (estimate)	Notes
Apocrypha of Jewish origin w/Christian accretions		
Sibylline Oracles	Various	Prophecies, emanating from the "sibyls" or divinely inspired seeresses; adapted by Jews to disseminate Jewish doctrines
Testaments of the Twelve Patriarchs	135 – 63 BC (Original)	Docetic components
The Ascension of Isaias	<100 AD	
Apocalypses of Elias" (Elijah)	??	
Sophonias (Zephaniah)	??	
Paralipomenon of Baruch	??	
Apocalypse of Moses	??	
Apocalypse of Esdras	??	
Testament of Abraham	??	
Testament of the Three Patriarchs	??	
Prayer of Joseph	??	
Prayer of Aseneth	??	
Marriage of Aseneth", (the wife of Joseph)	??	
Testaments of Job	??	Eastern origin – gnostic influences
Zacharias	??	Eastern origin – gnostic influences
Adam Books	??	Eastern origin – gnostic influences
Book of Creation	??	Eastern origin – gnostic influences
Story of Aphikia" (the wife of Jesus Sirach)	??	Eastern origin – gnostic influences

Christian Origin	Date (estimate)	Notes
Apocryphal gospels (sayings of Jesus)		
Pseudo-Matthew, et al	??	
Didascalia Apostolorum	230 AD	Genre of church orders (a la Didache)
The Protoevangelium Jacobi, or Infancy Gospel of James		
Gospel of St. Matthew	300–400 AD	Latin origin
Arabic Gospel of the Infancy		Arabic translation of Syriac original
Gospel of Gamaliel	400 AD	Coptic fragments
The Transitus Mariæ or Evangelium Joannis		Written in name of St. John
Judaistic and heretical gospels		
Gospel according to the Hebrews		Mentioned by Clement of Alexandria, Origen, Eusebius, and St. Epiphanius
Gospel According to the Egyptians		Gnostic work
Gospel of St. Peter		Docetic work
Gospel of St. Philip		Gnostic work
Gospel of St. Thomas		Gnostic work
Gospel of St. Bartholomew		Gnostic work
Gospel of the Twelve Apostles		Gnostic work
Gospel of St. Andrew		Gnostic work
Gospel of Barnabas		Gnostic work
Gospel of Thaddeus		Gnostic work
Gospel of Eve		Gnostic work
Gospel of Judas Iscariot		Gnostic work

Christian Origin	Date (estimate)	Notes
Pilate literature and other apocrypha concerning Christ		
Report of Pilate to the Emperor		
Acta Pilati (Gospel of Nicodemus)		
The Minor Pilate Apocrypha		
The Narrative of Joseph of Arimathea		
The Legend of Abgar		
Letter of Lentulus		
Apocryphal acts of the apostles		
Periodoi (Circuits)		
Praxeis (Acts) of the Apostles		
Historia Certaminis Apostolorum		
Acts of Sts. Peter and Paul		
Acts of St. Paul		
Acts of Paul and Thecla		Contains a description of St. Paul (accurate?)
Acts of St. Philip		
Acts of St. Matthew		
Teaching of Addai (Thaddeus)		
Acts of Simon and Jude		
The Acts of St. Barnabas		
Gesta Matthiæ		
Gnostic acts of the apostles		
Acts of St. Peter		

by, Michael J. Chenevey

Christian Origin	Date (estimate)	Notes
Acts of St. John		
Acts of St. Andrew		
The Acts and Martyrdom of St. Matthew		
Acts of St. Thomas		
Acts of St. Bartholomew		
Quasi–apostolic acts		
Acts of St. Mark	300–400 AD	Alexandrian origin, and written in the fourth or fifth century
Acts of St. Luke	399 AD	Coptic, not earlier than end of fourth
Acts of St. Timothy	>425 AD	Composed by an Ephesian after 425
Acts of St. Titus	400–700 AD	Cretan origin, between 400–700
Acts of Kanthippe and Polyxena		Connected with the legends about St. Paul and St. Andrew
Apocryphal doctrinal works		
Testamentum Domini Nostri Jesu		Monophysite origin
The Preaching of Peter or Kerygma Petri		Eusebius classes it as apocryphal
Two Ways or Judicium Petri		Of Jewish-Christian origin, and probably was based on the so-called "Epistle of Barnabas"
Preaching of Paul		Represented Christ as confessing personal sins, and forced by His mother to receive baptism.
Apocryphal epistles		
Pseudo-Epistles of the Blessed Virgin		Composed in Latin and at late dates
Pseudo-Epistle of St. Peter to St. James the Less		

Christian Origin	Date (estimate)	Notes
Pseudo-Epistles of St. Paul; Correspondence with the Corinthians		
Pseudo-epistle to the Laodiceans		
Pseudo-Correspondence of St. Paul and Seneca		Eight pretended letters from the Stoic philosopher Seneca, and six replies from St. Paul
Christian apocryphal apocalypses		
Apocalypse of the Testamentum D.N. Jesu Christi.		
The Apocalypse of Mary		
Apocalypses of St. Peter		
The Apocalypse of St. Paul		

APPENDIX F: ENGLISH BIBLE TRANSLATIONS

List of Incomplete Bibles (English Translations)

Bible	Translated sections	English variant	Year	Source	Notes
Aldhelm	Psalms (existence disputed).	Old English	late 7th or early 8th centuries	Vulgate	
Bede	Gospel of John (lost)	Old English	c. 735	Vulgate	
Psalters (12 in total), including the Vespasian Psalter and Eadwine's Canterbury Psalter.	English glosses of Latin psalters		9th century	Vulgate	
King Alfred	Pentateuch, including the Ten Commandments; possibly also the Psalms.	Old English	c. 900	Vulgate	
Aldred the Scribe	Northumbrian interlinear gloss on the Gospels in the Lindisfarne Gospels	Old English	950 to 970	Vulgate	
Farman	Gloss on the Gospel of Matthew in the Rushworth Gospels.	Old English	950 to 970	Vulgate	
Ælfric	Pentateuch, Book of Joshua, Judges.	Old English	c. 990	Vulgate	
Wessex Gospels	Gospels	Old English	c. 990	Vulgate	
Caedmon manuscript	A few English Bible verses	Old English	700 to 1000	Vulgate	

Bible	Translated sections	English variant	Year	Source	Notes
The Ormulum	Some passages from the Gospels and the Acts of the Apostles	Middle English	c. 1150	Vulgate	
A translation of Revelation	Book of Revelation	Middle English	Early 14th century	A French translation	
Rolle	Various passages, including some of the Psalms	Middle English	Early 14th century	Vulgate	
West Midland Psalms	Psalms	Middle English	Early 14th century	Vulgate	
A Catholic New Testament	New Testament	Middle English	c. 1400	Vulgate	
Caxton	Various passages	Middle English	1483 (Golden Legend) 1484 (The Book of the Knight of the Tower)	A French translation	

List of Partial English Bible Translations

Bible	Translated sections	English variant	Year	Source	Notes
Brenton's English Translation of the Septuagint	Old Testament	Modern English	1844	Septuagint	
The Emphatic Diaglott	New Testament	Modern English	1864	Greek text recension by Dr Johann Jakob Griesbach	
Twentieth Century New Testament	New Testament	Modern English	1904	Greek text of Westcott and Hort.	
James Moffat's 'The New Testament, A New Translation'	New Testament	Modern English	1913		

Bible	Translated sections	English variant	Year	Source	Notes
The New Testament, Confraternity Version	New Testament	Modern English	1941	Revision of the Challoner Revision of the Rheims New Testament.	
Spencer New Testament	New Testament	Modern English	1941	Greek text	The gospels were originally from the Vulgate, then the translation was re-started using the Greek
Kleist-Lilly New Testament	New Testament	Modern English	1956		
Phillips New Testament in Modern English	New Testament	Modern English	1958		
Wuest Expanded Translation	New Testament	Modern English	1961	Nestle-Aland Text	
Bible in Worldwide English	New Testament	Modern English	1969		

Bible	Translated sections	English variant	Year	Source	Notes
Confraternity Bible	NT (Confraternity Version), OT, various books from the Challoner revision of the Douay Old Testament.		1970		OT of the 1970 New American Bible.
Cotton Patch Series	New Testament	Modern English	1973		American idiomatic
God's New Covenant: A New Testament Translation	New Testament	Modern English	1989		
McCord's New Testament Translation of the Everlasting Gospel	New Testament	Modern English	1989		
The Unvarnished New Testament	New Testament	Modern English	1991		
International Standard Version	New Testament, with Old Testament in translation.	Modern English	1998		
The New Authorized Version	New Testament and parts of the Old Testament.	Modern English	1998	Revision of the King James Version.	
The Common Edition New Testament	New Testament	Modern English	1999		
The Apostles' Bible	Old Testament	Modern English	2004, 2007	Septuagint	A revision, by Paul W. Esposito, of Brenton's 1851 translation of the Septuagint

Bible	Translated sections	English variant	Year	Source	Notes
The LOLCat Bible	Most of the New and Old Testaments	LOLSpeak	2007		
The Orthodox Study Bible		Modern English	2008	Adds a new translation of the LXX to an existing translation of the NKJV in a single volume.	
The Comprehensive New Testament	New Testament	Modern English	2008	English Translation of the Nestle Aland 27th Edition of the Greek New Testament	
The Voice	New Testament	Modern English	2008		"A Scripture project to rediscover the story of the Bible."
The Fresh Agreement: God's Contract with Humanity	New Testament	Modern American-English	2011	3rd Edition of Robert Etienne (1550)	Brings the range and specificity of the modern vocabulary to the Traditional Greek text.

by, Michael J. Chenevey

Bible	Translated sections	English variant	Year	Source	Notes
The Open English Bible	New Testament	Modern English	2011 (Work in Progress)	Twentieth Century New Testament (English), Wescott-Hort (Greek)	CC-BY licensed version, edited from the public domain Twentieth Century New Testament
The Free Bible	Ruth, Obadiah and a few NT books		2011 (Work in Progress)		A Wiki translation, in progress
World English Bible	New Testament, with Old Testament in translation	Modern English	2011 (Work in Progress)	Majority Text	

List of Complete English Translation Bibles

Bible	English variant	Year	Source	Notes
Wycliffe's Bible (1380)	Middle English	1380	Latin Vulgate	
Wycliffe's Bible (1388)	Middle English	1388	Latin Vulgate	
Tyndale Bible	Jacobean English	1526 (New Testament) 1530 (Pentateuch)	Masoretic Text, Erasmus' third NT edition (1522), Martin Luther's 1522 German Bible.	Incomplete translation. Tyndale's other Old Testament work went into the Matthew's Bible (1537).

Bible	English variant	Year	Source	Notes
Coverdale Bible	Jacobean English	1535	Masoretic Text, the Greek New Testament of Erasmus, Vulgate, and German and Swiss-German Bibles	First complete Bible printed in English (Early Modern English)
Matthew's Bible	Jacobean English	1537	Masoretic Text, the Greek New Testament of Erasmus, the Vulgate, the Luther Bible, and a French version.	
Great Bible	Jacobean English	1539	Masoretic Text, Greek New Testament of Erasmus, the Vulgate, and the Luther Bible.	
Taverner's Bible	Jacobean English	1539		Minor revision of Matthew's Bible
Geneva Bible	Jacobean English	1557 (New Testament) 1560 (complete Bible)	Masoretic Text, Textus Receptus	First English Bible with whole of Old Testament translated direct from Hebrew texts
Bishops' Bible	Jacobean English	1568	Masoretic Text, Textus Receptus	
Douay-Rheims Bible	Jacobean English	1582 (New Testament) 1609–1610 (Old Testament)	Latin, Greek and Hebrew manuscripts	Old Testament completed in 1582, released in two parts in 1609 and 1610

Bible	English variant	Year	Source	Notes
King James Version	Jacobean English	1611	Masoretic Text, Textus Receptus, Tyndale 1526 NT, some Erasmus manuscripts, and Bezae 1598 TR.	
Algonquin (John Eliot)	Modern English	1661 NT 1663 (OT		First Bible version printed in America
Douay-Rheims Bible (Challoner Revision)	Modern English	1752	Clementine Vulgate	
Quaker Bible	Modern English	1764	Masoretic Text, Textus Receptus	
Thomson's Translation	Modern English	1808	Codex Vaticanus (according to the introduction in the reprint edition by S. F. Pells) of the Septuagint (but excluding the Apocrypha) and of the New Testament	
Webster's Revision	Modern English	1833		Revision of the King James Version.
James Murdock's Translation of the Syriac Peshitta	Modern English	1852	Syriac Peshitta	
Ferrar Fenton Bible	Modern English	1853	Masoretic Text and the Westcott and Hort Greek text	
Young's Literal Translation	Modern English	1862	Masoretic Text, Textus Receptus	
Julia E. Smith Parker Translation	Modern English	1876	Masoretic Text, Textus Receptus	

Bible	English variant	Year	Source	Notes
Revised Version	Modern English	1885		Revision of the King James Version, but with a critical New Testament text: Westcott and Hort 1881 and Tregelles 1857
Darby Bible	Modern English	1890	Masoretic Text, various critical editions of the Greek text (e.g. Tregelles, Tischendorf, Westcott and Hort)	
American Standard Version	Modern English	1901	Masoretic Text, Westcott and Hort 1881 and Tregelles 1857	
Rotherham's Emphasized Bible	Masoretic Text (Biblia Hebraica), Westcott-Hort Greek text	1902		
Jewish Publication Society of America Version Tanakh (Old Testament)	Modern English	1917	Masoretic Text	
Concordant Literal Version	Modern English	1926	A concordance of every form of every Greek word was made and systematized and turned into English.	
Moffatt, New Translation	Modern English	1926		
Lamsa Bible	Modern English	1933	Syriac Peshitta	
An American Translation	Modern English	1935	Masoretic Text, various Greek texts.	
Westminster Bible	Modern English	1936	Greek and Hebrew	

Bible	English variant	Year	Source	Notes
Bible in English	Modern English	1949		
Revised Standard Version	Modern English	1952	Masoretic Text, Nestle–Aland Greek New Testament.	
Knox's Translation of the Vulgate	Modern English	1955	Vulgate, with influence from the original Hebrew, Aramaic, and Greek.	
Berkeley Version	Modern English	1958		
New World Translation of the Holy Scriptures	Modern English	1950 (New Testament) 1960 (single volume complete Bible) 1984 (reference edition with footnotes)		
Children's King James Version	Modern English	1962	Revision of the King James Version.	by Jay P. Green
Judaica Press Tanakh (Old Testament).	Modern English	1963	Masoretic Text	
Amplified Bible	Modern English	1965	Revision of the American Standard Version	
Jerusalem Bible	Modern English	1966	From the original Hebrew, Aramaic, and Greek, with influence from the French La Bible de Jérusalem.	Roman Catholic
Revised Standard Version Catholic Edition	Modern English	1966		Revision of the Revised Standard Version.
Modern Language Bible	Modern English	1969		Also called "The New Berkeley Version"

Bible	English variant	Year	Source	Notes
New American Bible	Modern English	1970		
New English Bible	Modern English	1970	Masoretic Text, Greek New Testament	
King James II Version	Modern English	1971	Masoretic Text, Textus Receptus	by Jay P. Green, Sr.
The Living Bible	Modern English	1971	American Standard Version (paraphrase)	
New American Standard Bible	Modern English	1971	Masoretic Text, Nestle-Aland Text	
The Story Bible	Modern English	1971		A summary/paraphrase, by Pearl S. Buck
The Bible in Living English	Modern English	1972		
An American Translation	Modern English	1976	Masoretic Text, various Greek texts.	
Good News Bible	Modern English	1976	United Bible Society (UBS) Greek text	Formerly known as *Today's English Version*
New International Version	Modern English	1978	Masoretic Text, Nestle-Aland Greek New Testament (based on Westcott-Hort, Weiss and Tischendorf, 1862).	
New King James Version	Modern English	1982	Masoretic Text (Biblia Hebraica Stuttgartensia, 1983), Majority text (Hodges-Farstad, 1982)	
A Literal Translation of the Bible	Modern English	1985	Masoretic Text, Textus Receptus (Estienne 1550)	by Jay P. Green, Sr.

Bible	English variant	Year	Source	Notes
New Jerusalem Bible	Modern English	1985	From the original Hebrew, Aramaic, and Greek, with influence from the French La Bible de Jérusalem.	
New Jewish Publication Society of America Version. Tanakh (Old Testament)	Modern English	1985	Masoretic Text	
Recovery Version of the Bible	Modern English	1985		Revision of the American Standard Version and Darby Bible.
Christian Community Bible, English version	Modern English	1986	Hebrew and Greek (?)	
New Life Version	Modern English	1986		
Revised English Bible	Modern English	1987		Revision of the New English Bible.
Easy-to-Read Version	Modern English	1989		
New Revised Standard Version	Modern English	1989		Revision of the Revised Standard Version.
Modern King James Version	Modern English	1990	Masoretic Text, Textus Receptus	by Jay P. Green, Sr.
New Century Version	Modern English	1991		
Clear Word Bible	Modern English	1994		
Leeser Bible, Tanakh (Old Testament)	Modern English	1994	Masoretic Text	
The Living Torah and The Living Nach. Tanakh (Old Testament)	Modern English	1994	Masoretic Text	

Bible	English variant	Year	Source	Notes
Contemporary English Version	Modern English	1995		
God's Word	Modern English	1995		
ArtScroll Tanakh (Old Testament)	Modern English	1996	Masoretic Text	
New International Version Inclusive Language Edition	Modern English	1996	Revision of the New International Version.	
New Living Translation	Modern English	1996		
Complete Jewish Bible	Modern English	1998	Paraphrase of the Jewish Publication Society of America Version (Old Testament), and from the original Greek (New Testament).	
New International Reader's Version	Modern English	1998	New International Version (simplified syntax, but loss of conjunctions obscures meanings)	
Third Millennium Bible	Modern English	1998		Revision of the King James Version.
American King James Version	Modern English	1999	Revision of the King James Version	
English Jubilee 2000 Bible	Modern English	2000	Reina-Valera (1602 Edition)	
King James 2000 Version	Modern English	2000	Revision of the King James Version.	
EasyEnglish Bible	Modern English	2001		
English Standard Version	Modern English	2001	Revision of the Revised Standard Version. (Westcott-Hort, Weiss, Tischendorf Greek texts)	

Bible	English variant	Year	Source	Notes
The Message	Modern English	2002		
A Voice In The Wilderness Holy Scriptures	Modern English	2003	Masoretic Text, Textus Receptus	
Restored Name King James Version	Modern English.	2004		
Holman Christian Standard Bible	Modern English	2004	Masoretic Text, Nestle-Aland Text.	
Updated King James Version	Modern English	2004		
A Conservative Version	Modern English	2005		
New English Translation (NET Bible)	Modern English	2005	Masoretic Text, Nestle-Aland/United Bible Society Greek New Testament	
The Beloved and I	English Verse	2005		New Jubilees version of the Bible in English Verse by Thomas McElwain. Four volumes.
Today's New International Version	Modern English	2005	Masoretic Text (Biblia Hebraica Stuttgartensia, 1983), Nestle-Aland Greek text	Revision of the New International Version.
The Inclusive Bible	Modern English	2007	From the original Hebrew, Aramaic, and Greek	
Catholic Public Domain Version	Modern English	2009	Sixtus V and Clement VIII Latin Vulgate	by Ronald L. Conte Jr., in the public domain

Bible	English variant	Year	Source	Notes
The Work of God's Children Illustrated Bible	Modern English	2010	Revision of the Challoner Revision of the Douay-Rheims Bible.	by *The Work of God's Children*, in the public domain.

Source: http://en.wikipedia.org/wiki/List_of_English_Bible_translations

APPENDIX G: COMPARISON OF THE NEW TESTAMENT TO OTHER WORKS

Author	Work	Date	Earliest Copy	Approximate Time Span between original & copy	Number of Copies	Accuracy of Copies	Notes
Various	*New Testament*	1st Cent. A.D. (50-100 A.D.	2nd Cent. A.D. (c. 130 A.D. f.)	less than 100 years	5800	99.50%	
Homer	*Illiad*	900 B.C.	400 B.C.	500 years	643	95%	
Sophocles	*Various plays*	496-406 B.C.	1000 A.D.	1400 years	193	----	Sophocles wrote 123 plays during the course of his life, but only seven have survived in a complete form: Ajax, Antigone, Trachinian Women, Oedipus the King, Electra, Philoctetes and Oedipus at Colonus
Aristotle	*Corpus Aristotelicum*	384-322 B.C.	1100 A.D.	1400 years	49	----	
Livy	*Roman History*	59 BC-AD 17	----	?	20	----	142 books total, only 35 survive
Tacitus	*Histories*	circa 100 A.D.	1100 A.D.	1000 years	20	----	
Aristophanes	*Various plays*	450-385 B.C.	900 A.D.	1200 years	10	----	
Caesar	*Gallic War*	100-44 B.C.	900 A.D.	1000 years	10	----	
Euripides	*Various plays*	480-406 B.C.	1100 A.D.	1300 years	9	----	Ancient scholars thought that Euripides had written ninety-five plays, although four of those were probably written by Critias. Eighteen or nineteen of Euripides' plays have survived complete

by, Michael J. Chenevey

Author	Work	Date	Earliest Copy	Approximate Time Span between original & copy	Number of Copies	Accuracy of Copies	Notes
Demosthenes	Various orations	4th Cent. B.C.	1100 A.D.	800 years	8	- - - -	
Herodotus	History of Herodotus	480–425 B.C.	900 A.D.	1300 years	8	- - - -	
Suetonius	Lives of the Caesars (De vita Caesarum)	75–160 A.D.	950 A.D.	800 years	8	- - - -	
Thucydides	History of Thucydides	460–400 B.C.	900 A.D.	1300 years	8	- - - -	
Pliny (the Elder)	Natural History (Naturalis Historia)	61–113 A.D.	850 A.D.	750 years	7 (200 now?)	- - - -	Latin manuscript; 37 books in the History; Most of the copies now extant are from the middle ages, and filled with known errors from copyists
Plato	Dialogues	427–347 B.C.	900 A.D.	1200 years	7	- - - -	
Lucretius	On the Nature of Things (De Rerum Natura)	died 55 or 53 B.C.		1100 years	2	- - - -	Epic philosophical poem on Epicureanism. Written in Latin

Reference:
http://carm.org/manuscript-evidence

The above chart was adapted from three sources: 1) *Christian Apologetics*, by Norman Geisler, 1976, p. 307; 2) the article *"Archaeology and History attest to the Reliability of the Bible,"* by Richard M. Fales, Ph.D., in *The Evidence Bible*, Compiled by Ray Comfort, Bridge-Logos Publishers, Gainesville, FL, 2001, p. 163; and 3) *A Ready Defense*, by Josh McDowell, 1993, p. 45.

APPENDIX H: TEXTUAL CRITICISM APPLIED TO THE BIBLE

by, Michael J. Chenevey

INTRODUCTION

W hat is "textual criticism"? If you are or were an English or Literature major, then you already know what I am talking about. Here I am talking specifically about textual criticism applied to the Bible. Textual criticism is essentially a scientific approach to determining the origin of any piece of literature, and also determining any errors or discrepancies that may exist from the transmission of documents by hand. We all understand that the Bible was originally orally transmitted, then hand-written for many centuries in various languages before our modern Bible translations were printed. We have hand written copies of biblical manuscripts today. Textual criticism is an approach to understand the differences in those manuscripts.

The beginning point for this section was to find a view of New Testament (NT) textual criticism that is satisfactory from the vantage point of a high view of Scripture. To define this "high view," two statements are necessary. First, God communicated all the words of Scripture clearly and without contradiction. Second, as quoted directly from Wayne Grudem's *Systematic Theology*: "the inerrancy of Scripture means that Scripture in the original languages does not affirm anything that is contrary to fact."[96] A student of the Bible is early confronted by scholarly work that states unequivocally that certain passages of Scripture do not belong in the Bible. For example, the "long ending" of the Gospel of Mark is an example hotly debated for many years. It seems contradictory to hold a high view of Scripture as noted above and yet question the authenticity of many verses of Scripture. Does textual criticism provide accuracy without devaluing the authority of Scripture?

The doctrine of inerrancy of Scripture presupposes that the original text is known. Textual criticism concerns itself with ascertaining the original text. Textual criticism can be defined as follows: "textual criticism is the study of copies of any written work of which the autograph (the original) is unknown, with the purpose of ascertaining the original text."[97]

---

[96] Wayne Grudem, Systematic Theology, (Grand Rapids: Zondervan Publishing Co., 1991), p. 73-85.

[97] Harold Greenlee, Introduction to New Testament Textual Criticism, (Grand Rapids: William B. Eerdmans, 1964), p. 11.

Dr. Tregelles notes the same tension, namely that a textual critic questions the authenticity of certain verses of Scripture and therefore questioning inspiration of the material itself. The following quotation captures the conflict,

> *There is in some minds a kind of timidity with regard to Holy Scripture, as if all our notions of its authority depended on our knowing who was the writer of each particular portion; instead of simply seeing and owning that it was given forth from God, and that it is as much His as were the Commandments of the Law written by His own finger on the tables of stone.*[98]

The point at issue for Tregelles is the long ending of Mark, which he takes to be written by someone other than John Mark, but considers it no less inspired. Tregelles desires to retain Mark 16:9-20 as authentic without a question of authorship. John W. Burgon criticizes Tregelles here, though Burgon himself argues for the retention of 16:9-20, as too willing to dispense with his critical faculties for piety.

There are many Greek New Testament manuscripts and collected editions that piece together extant partial Greek Manuscripts to make whole Bibles. One can choose from a collection of Byzantine based manuscripts: Erasmus I edition (1516), Erasmus 5th edition (1535), Stephanus (1551), Textus Receptus (Elsevier, 1624), Byzantine/Majority. Or a person can opt for an Alexandrian based Greek New Testament as typified by a Wescott-Hort version and more recently with one of twenty-eight Nestle-Aland or four United Bible Society editions. This list is by no means exhaustive. It simply expresses the variety."[99]

There are over 5,300 Greek manuscripts, 8,000 Latin manuscripts, and 1,000 manuscripts of other languages that make up the New Testament. In contrast to the number of manuscripts found in the New Testament one need look no further in antiquity than the classical Greek writers whose works have been preserved since antiquity. J. Harold Greenlee states,

---

[98] John Burgon, The Last Twelve Verses According to the Gospel of Mark, (1959), p. 89.

[99] Barbara Aland and Kurt Aland, The Text of the New Testament: An Introduction to the Critical Editions and to the Theory and Practice of Modern Textual Criticism, (Grand Rapids: E. J. Brill, 1987), p. 34.

"Ancient Greek and Latin classics are known today, in some cases, from only one surviving manuscript."[100] At best, "Greek classical textual critics can claim hundreds of manuscripts and at worst a handful. The Greek Anthology and the Annals of Tacitus are known to have direct descent from earlier material. The plays of Aeschylus are known to have fifty manuscripts, the works of Sophocles one hundred, the works of Euripides, Cicero, Ovid, and Virgil a few hundred. A greater amount of manuscript evidence ensures a greater accuracy in the reconstruction of the original text. If only a handful of manuscripts are present, confidence in the accuracy could certainly be diminished. Further, the earliest extant New Testament manuscripts (MSS) were written much closer to the original writing than almost any other piece of ancient literature."[101]

J. Harold Greenlee notes the relationship between the manuscript evidence and inspiration, but it is important to see that the inspired, authoritative New Testament has come down through the centuries in a great multitude of ancient manuscripts that differ from one another in various details, that almost all of these manuscripts give us the Word of God, and that the exact wording of the original text can be determined only by studying the variants and applying sound principles to decide among them. The great multitude of manuscripts is a convincing proof for the inspiration of Scripture, nevertheless it is not satisfactory for all. It is often argued that the great number of variant readings among the New Testament manuscripts plays against the inspiration of Scripture.[102]

---

[100] J. Harold Greenlee, Scribes, Scrolls, & Scripture: A Student's Guide to New Testament Textual Criticism. (Grand Rapids: William B. Eerdmans Publishing Co., 1985), p. 3.

[101] J. Harold Greenlee, Introduction to New Testament Textual Criticism, p. 16.

[102] J. Harold Greenlee, Introduction to New Testament Textual Criticism, p. 15.

The point of contention is that the manuscripts do not agree exactly on every detail. In answer to this objection it may be noted that the manuscripts agree in most of their content. A second objection is that most of the variants do not affect the meaning of the text. What is not often taken into account by critics of Scripture's inspiration is that the business of textual criticism generally concerns itself with ". . . for the most part, small details and relatively minor matters."[103]

A few general principles must be mentioned in regard to the 'small details' and 'minor matters.' The methods of textual criticism offered by Kirsopp Lake follow this general pattern. (1) Study each individual manuscript by itself and correct obvious mistakes. (2) Compare manuscripts and arrange them into groups to distinguish an archetype. (3) Compare the archetypes and construct a provisional text of the archetype. (4) Subject the archetype texts to the process of conjectural emendation, i.e., an attempt to explain and emend all the passages that still seem corrupt.[104]

The first phase concerns itself with the 'small details' and 'minor matters.' 'Small details' often pertains to different spellings. 'Minor matters' generally regards scribal errors. Mistakes and corruptions fall under two classes: unintentional due to natural error and intentional due to a desire for improvement.[105] Unintentional alterations include dittography, homoioteleuton, haplography, and itacism. Dittography is the repetition of a letter, word or phrase when it should be written once. Homoioteleuton is the omission of a letter, word or phrase. Haplography, dittography's opposite, is the omission of a word actually repeated in the text. Itacism describes a copyist mistake of spelling or grammar. Intentional alterations include marginal notes, added traditional readings, grammatical improvements, harmonistic alterations, and dogmatic alterations.[106]

Phases two and three of New Testament textual criticism attempt to arrange manuscripts by genealogy. A modified view of B. H. Streeter's division of text-types is often the adopted one for discussion of text-types. Incidentally, it is important to note that the most significant contribution Streeter made is the principle of weighing manuscript (MSS) evidence rather than counting. Returning to genealogy, Streeter renames Hort's "a" text-type Byzantine, and the "b" text-type Alexandrian. Streeter disregards "g" (Caesarean) as a separate family and breaks "d" (Western) into four

---

[103] J. Harold Greenlee, Scribes, Scrolls, & Scripture, p. 55.

[104] Kirsopp Lake, The Text of the New Testament, (London: Billing & Sons Ltd., 1959), pp. 2-5.

[105] Kirsopp Lake, p. 3.

[106] Vincent Taylor, The Text of the New Testament, (London: Macmillan & Co. Ltd., 1963), p. 3.

groupings. The discussion that ensues will regard g as a separate family and d as a separate family.[107]

Genealogical grouping is viewed variously by scholars. Hort viewed genealogy as important and elevated b by arguing that some readings of b, particularly Vaticanus and its intimate kin, are superior. Therefore all MSS of b were superior. Von Soden agreed to the necessity of genealogy but disagreed in the historical reconstruction.[108] Streeter did much work in the g text-type belying his agreement to genealogical methodology.

Ernest Colwell points out that scholars have in various ways championed or repudiated particular text-types[i] or repudiated the arrangement of texts into text-types.[ii] Colwell advocates a moderate position that first determines a text-type in the largest group of sources that can objectively be identified by external evidence. The second point is to abandon efforts to establish the archetype text that Lake included as important. Third, one must recognize that there is a process in the development of the text-type resulting in gradual distinctiveness and uniformity. Fourth, the study of text-type and the resulting historical reconstruction does not precede study of individual texts but occurs simultaneously. Fifth, identify quantitative agreement with others in the text-type and qualitatively define it without resorting to construction of an archetype. Sixth, study the text-types book by book or section by section. Seventh, give priority to text-types that are frequently quoted. Eighth, begin with the earliest sources and work forward to the later sources. Ninth, recognize different values in different groupings.[109]

In view of the discussion of genealogy, James Borland sees a type of circular reasoning that biases selection of authentic readings. Borland briefly defines the rules of internal evidence as follows,

> (1) Prefer the reading that best explains the rise of other variants; (2) prefer the shorter reading; (3) prefer the more difficult reading; (4) prefer the reading most characteristic of the author.[110]

When a decision is difficult it is frequently regarded as safest to go with the best manuscript. Borland points out that Westcott and Hort reasoned that the best external

---

[107] Vincent Taylor, p. 57.

[108] Ernest Colwell, Studies in Methodology in Textual Criticism in the New Testament, (Netherlands: E. J. Brill, 1969), p. 2.

[109] Vincent Taylor, pp. 9, 15, 20-24.

[110] James Borland, "Re-examining New Testament Textual-Critical Principles and Practices used to Negate Inerrancy," Journal of the Evangelical Theological Society, Vol. 25, (Deerfield: Trinity Evangelical Divinity School, 1982), p. 501.

evidence was found in those manuscripts that contained the "best readings." The "best readings" were found in b, thus decisions can be made in favor of b. Borland questions whether b is so infallible.[111] In his article, Borland concerns himself with textual-critical studies' often hostile view to inerrancy of the Scriptures. Borland asks that textual criticism be altered to maintain a high view of Scripture. Borland states: "If we accept the inerrancy of the Scriptures and yet countenance a textual criticism that voids inerrancy, something is amiss — and I would suggest that it is not the Word of God that needs reconsideration but rather our principles of textual criticism."[112]

Before beginning the evidence Borland presents, it must be noted that it is very difficult to avoid noting Borland's bias throughout his article. For instance, Borland implies that textual critical study is Satanically influenced since in this modern era it uses 'highly technical tools' and 'computers.'[113] Returning to Borland's evidence, he cites two cases. Only one may be discussed for the sake of space.

Borland believes that this is one of the textual problems where scholars denigrate the inerrancy of Scripture. The first is Matthew 1:7,10 containing the kingly genealogy of Christ, which requires a decision between variant readings Asa verses Asaph. Nearly all textual critics regard Asaph the original whereas it is printed Asa in English Bibles (NAB, ASV, RSV, NASB) footnoting that Asaph is the original reading. On the side of Asaph are the following MSS: Codices X, B and C (4th and 5th century); minuscules 1, 13; cursives 700 and 1071 (12th century); MSS 209 (14th century), other language MSS K (4th or 5th), Coptic, Armenian, Ethiopic, and Georgian. In summary, about a dozen Greek MSS witness to Asaph. On the other hand hundreds of Greek witnesses exist for Asa. Uncials that contain Asa are E K L M S U V W G D and P dating fifth through the tenth centuries with a wide geographical distribution. Further, Washingtoneinsis and Regius (L) are often agreeable with Codex Vaticanus. In addition, there are hundreds of cursives that exhibit independence from the Byzantine text-type and other minuscules stating at the ninth century, which 33 of them align themselves constantly with X and B. The lectionaries stand behind the Asa reading as do old language (OL) MSS: Vercellensis (4th, AD), Vg, Curetonian, Sinaitic, Peshitta, Harclean and Palestinian (versions of Syriac).[114]

Borland interprets the data as follows. Only a preconceived idea could favor the dozen Alexandrian texts above the hundreds of Greek witness covering a vast geographical region and dating from fifth century (OL 4th) on up.[115] Borland believes it erroneous to favor any MSS text-type that does not have support throughout the

---

[111] James Borland, p. 500.

[112] James Borland, p.506.

[113] James Borland, p. 499.

[114] James Borland, pp. 501-2.

[115] James Borland, pp. 502-3.

ages and a widespread geographical region.[116]   Thus, Borland regards Asa as the overwhelming reading. Again, viewing Asa as the overwhelming favorite eliminates an inerrancy dilemma. Further, it vindicates Matthew as unconfused in his Jewish genealogy by faulting the scribal tradition for an error in some of the MSS but maintaining the correct rendering in most. Borland argues for a more balanced examination of both internal and external evidence, but especially call for a questioning of a manuscript considered 'best' that suggests errors in the autographs.

There is a dividing line between those who hold to the Byzantine textform or an eclectic textform usually favoring the Alexandrian textform. Maurice Robinson and William Pierpont, in defense of the Byzantine/Majority textform, argue that an historical reconstruction of textual transmission argues for the Byzantine/Majority over against the Alexandrian based eclectic textforms. The issue, Robinson and Pierpont believe, is Byzantine priority wherein a division in Byzantine-era manuscripts necessitated consultation of all other ancient manuscripts under the standard textual critical methods. Thus, Robinson and Pierpont offer an edited Byzantine/Majority Greek New Testament as the closest to the autographs.[117]

HISTORICAL OVERVIEW OF TEXTUAL CRITICS

The division indicated necessitates a historical overview. The following is not intended to be exhaustive nor is intended to be revisionist. What is included here is that which leads up to the tension between eclecticists and Byzantine prioritists.

In the fifteenth century biblical scholars were more concerned with the Latin Vulgate. The first Latin edition was printed in 1456 (Guttenberg Bible). In 1514, Cardinal Ximenes of Spain began the preparation of a Greek New Testament. The New Testament was printed that year (Complutensian Polyglot) but publication was delayed because the pope would not approve it until the Old Testament volumes were printed. The first, however, to be published was begun by Erasmus in September, 1516 with six MSS. Seven months later in March 1516, the first Greek New Testament was published (Erasmus). In 1546, Robert Estienne published the Stephanus Greek New Testament using fifteen manuscripts and the third edition contained variant readings in a critical apparatus. Theodore Beza, a French Protestant scholar, published nine

---

[116] James Borland, p. 506.

[117] William Pierpont and Maurice Robinson, The New Testament in the Original Greek According to the Byzantine / Majority Textform. (Atlanta: The Original Word Publishers, 1991), p. xxvi-xlii.

editions of the Greek NT essentially in the Erasmus-Stephanus version. In 1624 through 1678, the Elzevir brothers of Holland dominated the scene with seven editions. The second edition (1633) became the standard text for the continental United States. This version received the title 'Textus Receptus' (received text).[118]

John Mill published a 3rd edition of the Textus Receptus (1707) with a few changes and a critical apparatus with readings of 78 MSS and some Patristic evidence. Johannes Albert Bengel published a text in 1734 deserting the Textus Receptus when other preferable readings were already in print. Bengel began a classification system calling them African or Asiatic. John Jacob Wetstein published the Textus Receptus with the true readings in the apparatus designating uncials by capital letters and minuscules by Arabic numbers. Johann Salomo Semler separated Bengel's classification of witnesses into Alexandrian, Western, and Eastern families. Semler's pupil, Johann Jakob Griesbach published three editions and collated large numbers of manuscripts. Karl Lachmann, a classicist, was the first to depart from the Textus Receptus in 1831 and in a second edition delineated principles of textual criticism that stood behind his 'critical text.' Samuel Prideaux Tregelles also collated manuscripts, published his own critical text (1857-79) with a critical apparatus and explanation of textual critical principles. Constantine Tischendorf discovered many manuscripts, including Codex Sinaiticus (X), and published eight editions unequaled in comprehensiveness. Tischendorf included citations of Greek manuscripts, versions, and patristic evidence. Perhaps the two most important textual critical scholars, Brooke Foss Westcott and Fenton John Antony Hort, coupled together and published a twenty eight year work in two volumes under the title The New Testament in the Original Greek (1881-1882).[119] Westcott and Hort, building on the foundations of their predecessors at last vanquished the Textus Receptus by ". . . the thoroughness with which they explained their views in their volume of introduction, and the fact that their text was printed in a handy, easily usable volume without the added bulk of an extensive critical apparatus."[120]

Westcott and Hort postulated the following method for determining the critical text: (1) study individual readings on the basis of intrinsic probability; (2) evaluate the individual witnesses; (3) determine the family groupings of the witnesses; and (4) return to the individual readings to confirm or revise conclusions. Intrinsic probability relates to internal evidence (e.g., congruence of language with author). External evidence related to the testimony of MSS, versions, patristic citations, etc. Westcott and Hort divided MSS witnesses into four groups: (1) most of the minuscules,

---

[118] J. Harold Greenlee, Introduction to New Testament Textual Criticism, pp. 69-72.

[119] J. Harold Greenlee, Introduction to New Testament Textual Criticism, pp. 73-7.

[120] J. Harold Greenlee, Introduction to New Testament Textual Criticism, p. 77.

later uncials, later versions (4th century and beyond) designated 'Syrian'; (2) a small group of witnesses (e.g., x, B) designated the 'Neutral Text'; (3) witnesses that composed the 'Neutral' group but differed with codex B was designated 'Alexandrian'; (4) a small group of MSS (e.g., D, D2), Old Latin version, and most Fathers of second and third centuries designated 'Western.'[121]

Westcott and Hort incited a final Textus Receptus defense by F. H. A. Scrivener, and by J. W. Burgon coupled with Edward Miller. Burgon and Miller argued a threefold defense: (1) God would not permit His church a corrupt text; (2) it is unnecessary to set aside hundreds of later manuscripts in favor of a few early witnesses; (3) the traditional text was actually older and intrinsically superior to the younger.[122] Another scholar, Wilbur N. Pickering adopts Burgon and Miller's argument in criticism of the Westcott and Hort theory. Maurice A. Robinson and William G. Pierpont also prioritize a Byzantine textform and delineate this in The New Testament in the Original Greek: According to the Byzantine/Majority Textform.

W. N. Pickering's criticisms of the Westcott-Hort theory are extensive. Pickering first uses one of Hort's letters to indicate an obvious agenda the youthful Hort (age 23) had against the Textus Receptus before he had done any serious study. Hort's goal was to replace the "villainous Textus Receptus" in one year with a revision of the Greek New Testament. It took twenty-eight years to finish the New Testament but it did ultimately dethrone the Textus Receptus.[123]

Hort used a genealogical method to overthrow the numerical superiority of manuscripts the Textus Receptus held over his "Neutral," "Alexandrian," and "Western" families. Hort's supposition was that one copy could be copied many times over and yet not be the correct one. Thus, Textus Receptus became one competing text-type called "Syrian" among other text-types. With equal chance at authenticity it had to be determined what families represented a more original reading.[124]

Using the term "conflation" to describe a reading existing as a mixture of other earlier manuscripts was Hort's attempt to discredit the "Syrian" readings. Scholars such as Vincent Taylor and Kirsopp Lake believed this to be a cornerstone argument for the Westcott-Hort (W-H) theory. Further discrediting the "Syrian" readings was Hort's contention that Syrian readings did not exist prior to the middle of the third

---

[121] J. Harold Greenlee, Introduction to New Testament Textual Criticism, pp. 79-80.

[122] J. Harold Greenlee, Introduction to New Testament Textual Criticism, pp. 81-2.

[123] Wilbur Pickering, The Identity of the New Testament Text, (Nashville: Thomas Nelson Inc., Publishers, 1977), p. 31.

[124] Wilbur Pickering, pp. 34-6.

century. Lake and Kenyon also noted the key role of this argument in the W-H theory.[125]

Another discrediting argument Hort used was the "Lucianic Recension" in which Hort tentatively suggested the church Father Lucian as a senior editor masterminding a revision process resulting in the overwhelming numbers in the "Syrian" family.[126]

Pickering's attack on the genealogical method marshaled the contemporary scholarship [iii] who considered the W-H genealogical method inapplicable to the New Testament. Westcott and Hort are now criticized for not providing evidence or the application of the method on the New Testament. Further honing in on text-types Parvis and Wikgren find no basis for generalizations about a "Byzantine" (Syrian) text. Zuntz discredits the idea that codex B is a 'neutral' text or that the "Western" text is the dominant 2nd century text. Klijn doubts whether grouping MSS in families (i.e., Alexandrian, Caesarean, Western, and Byzantine) can be maintained. H. C. Hoskier's massive collations forced his conclusion that absolutely no confidence could rest on the teachings of Dr. Hort.[127]

As regards conflation Pickering notes the ludicrous proposition that eight examples in two Gospels (Mark and Luke) could characterize a supposed family of MSS. Burgon has questioned most of the eight. E. A. Hutton's work, An Atlas of Textual Criticism, listed 821 instances of conflation. Out of all that, Pickering states that only a few cases of Syrian conflation[iv] may be culled. Further, Hort's claim that inversions[v] (conflations of other text-types with the Syrian) were nonexistent is not true. Finally, Lake questioned whether in a triple variant the longer reading could be assumed a conflation of two shorter readings apart from Patristic evidence.[128]

Regarding Syrian readings before Chrysostom, a collation of Chrysostom's text shows that it contains no appreciable difference of Textus Receptus variants against the Neutral text (Western and Alexandrian). Origen also had no settled text; he sided with the Textus Receptus 460 times and the Neutral text with Western combined totaled 491 times. Irenaeus sided with the Textus Receptus 63 times and the Western plus Neutral 41 times. Hyppolytus cited two long passages (1 Thess. 4:13-17, 2 Thess. 2:1-12) that agree with Textus Receptus readings. Miller's study concludes that Origen uses Textus Receptus 2:1 compared to Western combined with Neutral. By combining Origen, Justin Martyr, Heracleon, Clement of Alexandria, and Tertullian results in a 1.33:1 ratio in favor of the Textus Receptus. There is much more evidence unexamined

---

[125] Wilbur Pickering, p. 104.

[126] Wilbur Pickering, p. 37.

[127] Wilbur Pickering, pp. 44-50.

[128] Wilbur Pickering, pp. 58-62.

here [vi], but it is sufficient to describe the case that Syrian readings in fact predate 350 AD.[129]

Another argument Pickering uses is Papyri vindication of Byzantine readings. The strength of this argument is found in the Papyri's dating in the 2nd century. P46 agrees with a number of previously discarded Byzantine readings. Thirteen percent of Byzantine readings considered late have been proved by Papyrus Bodmer II to be early readings. H. A. Sturz conservatively estimated 150 distinctive Byzantine readings supported by Papyri. Colwell even places Byzantine readings in this early second century: "most of its [Byzantine New Testament] readings existed in the second century."[130]

The final argument Pickering musters to destroy the Westcott-Hort theory is the demolition of the Lucianic Recension theory. Hort postulated that the church Father Lucian worked with copyists and created a recension of which the Syrian text is made. Again Pickering needs only to survey scholarly literature. Burgon scoffs since there is simply not a trace of historical evidence.[131]

The conclusion of the matter is that Westcott and Hort's theory is destroyed and as Epp states no theory has replaced it. Aland and Colwell agree that apart from a reconstruction of the history of transmission textual criticism attempts the impossible.[132]

PICKERING'S HISTORICAL RECONSTRUCTION

Wilbur N. Pickering reconstructs the historical textual transmission first acknowledging that from the time of Irenaeus there is no doubt that the New Testament writings are considered Scripture.[133] The early Fathers were soon alarmed by heretics who would dare pervert the sayings of the Lord. Irenaeus adjured any copyist of his own work by the God who 'judges the living and the dead' to carefully copy and correct any possible errors in copying. The early Fathers' concern for Scripture necessitates even more care in handling the Scriptures, which holds greater esteem to the Fathers than their own works. Pickering then goes on to maintain that

---

[129] Wilbur Pickering, pp. 62-74.

[130] Ernest C. Colwell, What Is the Best New Testament? (Chicago: The University of Chicago Press, 1952), p. 70.

[131] Wilbur Pickering, p. 88-91.

[132] Wilbur Pickering, pp. 93-99.

[133] Wilbur Pickering, pp. 100-4.

Tertullian (circa 208 AD) indicated that the "authentic writings are read" meaning at the very least that the copies were faithful copies of the autographs.[134]

Pickering places possession of the autographs in regions. Asia Minor held John, Galatians, Ephesians, Colossians, 1 Timothy, 2 Timothy, Philemon, 1 Peter, 1 John, 2 John, 3 John, and Revelation. Greece held 1 Corinthians, 2 Corinthians, Philippians, 1 Thessalonians, 2 Thessalonians, and Titus. Rome held Mark and Romans. Luke, Acts, and 2 Peter, were held at Rome or Asia Minor. Matthew and James were held by Asia Minor or Palestine. Jude was possibly held by Asia Minor. This leaves eighteen autographs and possibly twenty-four in the collective region of Greece and Asia Minor (called the Aegean region); Rome held two to seven; Palestine held up to three; Alexandria held zero.[135]

The making of copies commenced immediately.[136] Evidence of this norm includes Peter's acknowledgment of a Pauline Corpus and the common practice of circular letter reproduction typified by Polycarp's sending a collection of Ignatius's letters to the Philippian church. There was free travel and exchange between the churches, which practiced weekly Scripture readings. Any questions of accuracy could still be checked against faithful copies of the autographs if they had perished (200 AD). Proliferation of copies under normal probability leads to majority agreement among texts and the high rate of agreement is accounted for by the careful treatment of the sacred Scriptures. It would take cataclysmic circumstances to overthrow such statistical probability. The minority manuscripts constitute 10-20% and ". . . disagree as much (or more) among themselves as they do with the majority" and the reason is the aberrant textforms introduced by heretics.[137] Pickering gives the orthodox Father, Gaius, who named four heretics who altered texts and multiplied their copies as an example of how aberrant textual transmission took place.[138]

Pickering describes the stream of transmission as a triangle broadening out at the base in the later years. Within that triangle are the MSS with minor variations. Outside the triangle are those whose transmissions are described as abnormal. Thus, Pickering finds the Majority Text dominating the stream of transmission.

---

[134] Wilbur Pickering, pp. 104-7.
[135] Wilbur Pickering, p. 105.
[136] Wilbur Pickering, p. 104-7.
[137] Wilbur Pickering, p. 112.
[138] Wilbur Pickering, p. 109.

TEXTUAL CRITICISM TODAY

Eldon Jay Epp, in his article "A Continuing Interlude in New Testament Textual Criticism," defends his 1973 Hatch Memorial Lecture from Kurt Aland. Epp asserted that the field of textual criticism was in need of a methodology and an understanding of the history. In 1990, Epp voices again the need for theories dealing with the manuscript witnesses and a historical reconstruction. Aland believes Epp to be naive in that in Aland's opinion it is impossible. No longer do New Testament textual critics work with genealogies, nor is the Westcott-Hort theory accepted. Epp goes on then to explain that there is a strikingly large amount of data today and no workable theories or advances in our understanding of that data.[139]

Aland supplies a theory called the local-genealogical method. The local-genealogical method approach ignores family groupings and compares only variation units. This requires that "in each locale, then, the genealogy of variants is constructed so as to isolate that variant reading from which all the others successively are to be explained, at the same time taking into full consideration all applicable internal criteria."[140] Epp shows concern over Aland's notion of the "expert practitioner" who is so familiar with the variants that ". . . at the sight of the variants and their attestation at a given place generally will very soon be clear as to where the original text is to be sought."[141] Epp notes the subjectivity engendered by such an intuitional approach. Epp concedes that the only method available today is Aland's local-genealogical method but maintains that it is merely a temporary until something better than slippery eclecticism or myopic variant-by-variant assessment is grounded on the solid rock of historical reconstruction.[142]

RELATIONSHIP TO INERRANCY

If 80% of the textual tradition is useless, namely the Byzantine tradition, then it is arguably less a numerical superiority to the works of Latin and Greek antiquity.

---

[139] Eldon Jay Epp, New Testament Textual Criticism Past, Present, and Future: Reflections on the Alands' Text of the New Testament, Harvard Theological Review, Vol. 82, (Cambridge: Harvard Divinity School, 1989), p. 135.

[140] Ibid., p. 141.

[141] Ibid., p. 142.

[142] Ibid., p. 151.

Further, the agreement between the text-types left is greatly decreased. In other words, to state that there is 90% agreement among MSS as a proof for inspiration necessitates the redemption of 80% of MS witnesses.

The case to be concluded here is that no text-type or form exists apart from its agreement with other Papyri, MSS and church Fathers. Current editions still largely compare with Westcott-Hort in that their primary reliance is upon three manuscripts (x B d). One cannot justify a three manuscript New Testament with consultation of others when they disagree. The theories today simply do not back up such methodology, nor does any evidence purport to. Current methods really do not rely upon the church Fathers for attestation. One may argue that they are included in the critical apparatus as witnesses. Nevertheless, modern methods of textual criticism will often decide the matter long before the church Fathers are consulted, thus the Fathers are merely icing on the cake.

Excellent scholars are beginning to acknowledge that there is not a current theory that is workable. The present theories seem to present more problems than solutions. Especially regarding inerrancy there is a problem created when errors are pointed out where they do not agree with a handful of MSS (x B d). Modern methodology must be moored, in this author's humble opinion, to the idea that the manuscripts attest to inerrant autographs. The vast number alone is proof that the autographs are inerrant. Hence, any methodology that advances a few manuscripts against many over a vast geographical region must be questioned. The suggestion here is that a new methodology begin with the assumption that the autographs are inerrant and that the number of witnesses attest to that fact. Proceeding from there is the only safe ground.

Further, as many have noted before, textual criticism must be anchored firmly to the bedrock of historical reconstruction. Current methods do not do this, though they may agree that it is needful. So far, Pickering's reconstruction is the best offered though it does not seem readily accepted. The only exception known is found in the work of Pierpont and Robinson who offer a similar account. Also, it seems more reasonable to accept Pickering's stream of transmission, which concurs with the proposition above. The smaller the attestation, unless convincingly proved a scribal error or falsification, the more likely the reading is to be considered aberrant. Less weight should be given to subjective interpretation of internal evidence and more weight given to Church Fathers and the stream of transmission. Under these guiding principles it is highly likely that the form of the text will be largely Byzantine, however, that is only if one still regards the genealogy as useful. The end result of that would perhaps please Textus Receptus enthusiasts or those wedded to the King James. This author cares little about that and in fact does not relish the idea of reading the King James Bible. What is important here is not what English version one prefers, but that the most accurate New Testament that reflects the inerrant autographs be developed for sound exegesis, teaching and reading. English translations can be made.

Further, if the textform is more representative of the whole, then this entire business of questioning the authenticity of certain verses will greatly diminish. Upon this basis a greater confidence is produced in those who exegete, teach, or read the Scriptures.

BIBLIOGRAPHY FOR TEXTUAL CRITICISM

Barbara Aland and Kurt Aland, The Text of the New Testament: An Introduction to the Critical Editions and to the Theory and Practice of Modern Textual Criticism, (Grand Rapids: E. J. Brill, 1987).

James Borland, "Re-examining New Testament Textual-Critical Principles and Practices used to Negate Inerrancy," Journal of the Evangelical Theological Society, Vol. 25, (Deerfield: Trinity Evangelical Divinity School, 1982).

John Burgon, The Last Twelve Verses According to the Gospel of Mark, (1959).

Ernest Colwell, Studies in Methodology in Textual Criticism in the New Testament, (Netherlands: E. J. Brill, 1969).

Ernest C. Colwell, What Is the Best New Testament? (Chicago: The University of Chicago Press, 1952).

Eldon J. Epp, "Why Does New Testament Textual Criticism Matter?," Expository Times 125 no. 9 (2014).

Eldon Jay Epp, New Testament Textual Criticism Past, Present, and Future: Reflections on the Alands' Text of the New Testament, Harvard Theological Review, Vol. 82, (Cambridge: Harvard Divinity School, 1989).

Eldon J. Epp, A Continuing Interlude in New Testament Textual Criticism, in Harvard Theological Review. Vol. 73., (Cambridge: Harvard Divinity School, 1990).

Harold Greenlee, Introduction to New Testament Textual Criticism, (Grand Rapids: William B. Eerdmans, 1964)

J. Harold Greenlee, Scribes, Scrolls, & Scripture: A Student's Guide to New Testament Textual Criticism. (Grand Rapids: William B. Eerdmans Publishing Co., 1985).

Peter J. Gurry, The Number of Variants in the Greek New Testament: A Proposed Estimate, (in New Testament Studies 62.1, 2016).

Kirsopp Lake, The Text of the New Testament, (London: Billing & Sons Ltd., 1959).

Scot McKnight, The Byzantine Text-Type and New Testament Textual Criticism by Harry A. Sturz: A Book Review, Trinity Journal, Vol. 5-6, (Deerfield: Trinity Evangelical Divinity School, 1984).

Bruce Metzger, The Text of the New Testament: its Transmission, Corruption, and Restoration, (New York: Oxford University Press, 1964).

Wilbur Pickering, The Identity of the New Testament Text, (Nashville: Thomas Nelson Inc., Publishers, 1977).

William Pierpont and Maurice Robinson, The New Testament in the Original Greek According to the Byzantine / Majority Textform. (Atlanta: The Original Word Publishers, 1991).

Vincent Taylor, The Text of the New Testament, (London: Macmillan & Co. Ltd., 1963).

Gene Ulrich, The Dead Sea Scrolls and the Origins of the Bible, (Grand Rapids: William B. Eerdmans Publishing Company, 1999).

B.F. Westcott, and F. J. A. Hort, Introduction to the New Testament in the Original Greek, (Peabody, Massachusetts: Hendrickson Publishers, Inc., 1988, Reprinted from 1882).

BIBLIOGRAPHY

Barbara Aland and Kurt Aland, The Text of the New Testament: An Introduction to the Critical Editions and to the Theory and Practice of Modern Textual Criticism, (Grand Rapids: E. J. Brill, 1987).

Klaus Beyer, The Aramaic Language: its distribution and subdivisions. John F. Healey (trans.), (Göttingen: Vandenhoeck und Ruprecht, 1986).

James Borland, "Re-examining New Testament Textual-Critical Principles and Practices used to Negate Inerrancy," Journal of the Evangelical Theological Society, Vol. 25, (Deerfield: Trinity Evangelical Divinity School, 1982).

George Braziller, Scrolls from the Dead Sea, (New York: George Braziller, Inc., 1993).

F.F. Bruce, The Canon of Scripture, (Downer's Grove, IL: InterVarsity Press, 1988).

John Burgon, The Last Twelve Verses According to the Gospel of Mark, (1959).

Ernest C. Colwell, Studies in Methodology in Textual Criticism in the New Testament, (Netherlands: E. J. Brill, 1969).

Ernest C. Colwell, What Is the Best New Testament? (Chicago: The University of Chicago Press, 1952).

Bart D. Ehrman: Misquoting Jesus: The Story Behind Who Changed the Bible and Why, (New York: HarperCollins, 2005).

Otto Eissfeldt, The Old Testament, An Introduction, (New York: Harper and Row, 1965).

Eldon J. Epp, "Why Does New Testament Textual Criticism Matter?," Expository Times 125 no. 9 (2014).

Eldon J. Epp, New Testament Textual Criticism Past, Present, and Future: Reflections on the Alands' Text of the New Testament, Harvard Theological Review, Vol. 82, (Cambridge: Harvard Divinity School, 1989).

Eldon J. Epp, A Continuing Interlude in New Testament Textual Criticism, in Harvard Theological Review. Vol. 73., (Cambridge: Harvard Divinity School, 1990).

Meskel and the Ethiopians. Ethiopian Orthodox Tewahedo Church (EOTC) Publication Committee, September, 2015.

Adam Fox, John Mill and Richard Bentley: A Study of the Textual Criticism of the New Testament 1675–1729 (Oxford: Basil Blackwell, 1954).

Norman Geisler and Peter Bocchino, Unshakeable Foundations, (Minneapolis, MN: Bethany House Publishers, 2001).

J. Harold Greenlee, Introduction to New Testament Textual Criticism, (Grand Rapids: William B. Eerdmans, 1964)

J. Harold Greenlee, Scribes, Scrolls, & Scripture: A Student's Guide to New Testament Textual Criticism. (Grand Rapids: William B. Eerdmans Publishing Co., 1985).

Wayne Grudem, Systematic Theology, An Introduction to Biblical Doctrine, (Grand Rapids: Zondervan Publishing Co., 1991).

Peter J. Gurry, The Number of Variants in the Greek New Testament: A Proposed Estimate, (in New Testament Studies 62.1, 2016).

Louis Edward Ingelbart, Press Freedoms: A Descriptive Calendar of Concepts, Interpretations, Events, and Courts Actions, from 4000 B.C. to the Present, p. 40, (Westport, CT: Greenwood Publishing, 1987).

Irenaeus, Against Heresies, Book III.

Flavius Josephus, Antiquities of the Jews, Book XII, ii

Andreas Juckel, A Guide to Manuscripts of the Peshitta New Testament, Hugoye Journal of Syriac Studies, (The Syriac Institute and Gorgias Press, 2012).

Michael Keevak, The Story of a Stele: China's Nestorian Monument and Its Reception in the West, 1625–1916, (Hong Kong: Hong Kong University Press, 2008)

Kirsopp Lake, The Text of the New Testament, (London: Billing & Sons Ltd., 1959).

William Sanford LaSor, Old Testament Survey, (Grand Rapids, MI: Eerdmans, 1996).

Scot McKnight, The Byzantine Text-Type and New Testament Textual Criticism by Harry A. Sturz: A Book Review, Trinity Journal, Vol. 5-6, (Deerfield: Trinity Evangelical Divinity School, 1984).

Bruce Metzger, The Text of the New Testament: its Transmission, Corruption, and Restoration, (New York: Oxford University Press, 1964).

John Mill, Novum Testamentum Graecum, cum lectionibus variantibus MSS (Oxford, 1707).

Eberhard Nestle, Einführung in das Griechische Neue Testament, (University of California Libraries, 1909).

Robert C. Newman, The Council of Jamnia and the Old Testament Canon, 1983, website: http://www.ibri.org/RRs/RR013/13jamnia.html

Wilbur Pickering, The Identity of the New Testament Text, (Nashville: Thomas Nelson Inc., Publishers, 1977).

William Pierpont and Maurice Robinson, The New Testament in the Original Greek According to the Byzantine / Majority Textform. (Atlanta: The Original Word Publishers, 1991).

Philip Schaff and Henry Wace, Eds., Early Church Fathers series, (Buffalo, NY: Christian Literature Publishing Co., 1892).

Philo of Alexandria, De Vita Moysis, II, vi

Orpa Slapak, The Jews of India: A Story of Three Communities, The Israel Museum, Jerusalem. 2003.

Douglas Stuart, Old Testament Exegesis, (Philadelphia: The Westminster Press, 1980).

Vincent Taylor, The Text of the New Testament, (London: Macmillan & Co. Ltd., 1963).

Gene Ulrich, The Dead Sea Scrolls and the Origins of the Bible, (Grand Rapids: William B. Eerdmans Publishing Company, 1999).

James C. Vanderkam, The Dead Sea Scrolls Today, (Grand Rapids: William B. Eerdmans Publishing Company, 1994).

B.F. Westcott, and F. J. A. Hort, Introduction to the New Testament in the Original Greek, (Peabody, Massachusetts: Hendrickson Publishers, Inc., 1988, Reprinted from 1882).

Robert Louis Wilken, The First Thousand Years: A Global History of Christianity, (New Haven and London: Yale University Press, 2013).

INDEX

ABOUT THE AUTHOR

Michael Chenevey has spent over seventeen years as a pastor, church planter, associate pastor, small group leader and director of adult teaching ministries serving several local congregations. He holds a Bachelor of Science degree in geology from University of Mount Union in Alliance, Ohio, a Master of Science degree in geology from University of Nevada, Reno, and a Master of Divinity from Oral Roberts University in Tulsa, Oklahoma. Mike has worked as a mining geologist, an Information Technology and Geographic Information System consultant, and an account manager, and is a licensed minister with the Assemblies of God. He has been married to Kristina for over twenty-four years and they have three grown sons and a daughter-in-law.

69799454R00083

Made in the USA
Lexington, KY
07 November 2017